Aesthetics of prose

Arne Melberg

Unipub 2008

©Unipub AS 2008

ISBN 978-82-7477-374-5

Contact info Unipub:
T: + 47 22 85 33 00
F: + 47 22 85 30 39
E-mail: post@unipub.no
www.unipub.no

Publisher: Oslo Academic Press, Unipub Norway
This book has been produced with financial support from
ILOS, University of Oslo.
Printed in Norway: AIT e-dit AS, Oslo 2008

All rights reserved. No part of this publication may be reproduced or
transmitted, in any form or by any means, without permission

Arne Melberg
Aesthetics of prose

In this book I am collecting my considerations from the last few years on the phenomenon and the aesthetics of prose. This means that not only am I writing new material, but also re-using, adjusting and conforming quite a lot of text that has already been published in the Scandinavian languages. Some elements from articles in English have also been re-used, as will be mentioned in due time. In the first section, I present two of my favorite god-fathers of modern prose: Montaigne and Nietzsche. In the second section, I am considering some versions of prose and modernity through two other favorites: Benjamin and Adorno. Finally, I look at modern prose through the development of the modern prose-poem. In the third section, I assemble examples from two vital sections of modern prose on the boundaries of literary fiction: travel writing and life writing. In the final section I make four shorter extensions, the first three extending the idea of prose in different directions while problematizing history and memory. The first deals with photos in literary fiction (as used by W. G. Sebald in particular); the second with the "design" of human identity in some modern arts; the third with the idea of appearance in modern aesthetic theory. In the last extension I make a short summary of the aesthetics of prose.

I am taking my examples from a wide range of literature. Whenever possible I use existing English translations for quotations. When I haven't been able to find a translation, I have provided my own.

Oslo, May 2008
Arne Melberg

Contents

I Prose: The Tradition

Montaigne: Essayistic Prose 9
Nietzsche: Performative Prose 29

II Prose and Modernity

Benjamin: Prose and Porosity 51
Adorno: Concentric Prose 67
Prose as Poetry, Poetry as Prose 81

III Prose on the Borderlines of Fiction

Sightseeing: Travel Writing 99
Exiles: life writing 127

IV Extensions

Sebald's photographic prose 159
Human design 167
Aesthetic Appearances 171
Aesthetics of Prose 177

Index 179

I Prose: The Tradition

Montaigne: Essayistic Prose

Withdrawal

In 1570, Michel de Montaigne resigned from his job as a tribunal lawyer in Bordeaux. He had had this office for fifteen years, shall soon become thirty-eight years old and believes it is about time to withdraw to his estate in the countryside. The estate bears his own name, Montaigne, and looks (as it still does today) medieval: a yard surrounded by buildings, two towers at the entrance. One of these towers is his; the other one is his wife's. The tower has three floors: on the ground floor, a small chapel; on the second floor, a room where Montaigne sleeps when he wishes to be alone; at the top, is the biggest room, with light from three windows. Here Montaigne sets out his desk and substantial library. He carves quotes into the beams from his favorite writers. (That is according to the Montaigne myth: perhaps the carvings came later?) Montaigne wants a place where he can feel undisturbed by the world and where he can dedicate himself to his own thoughts and to himself. He has come to the age of thirty-eight and wants to save whatever is left of "this tail-end of life," *ce bout de vie* (as he calls it in the essay "On Solitude"), for himself.[1] He wishes to enjoy what the Renaissance humanists called *otium* – free time and space – although it should be an *otium cum litteris*, a free space filled with literature. Montaigne wants to go behind his public persona to cultivate his private person. The setting for his retreat is his famous tower, its top-room with his library is his *arrière-boutique* as he calls it, his "inner room" behind the public room of duties: "We should set aside a room, just for ourselves, at the back of the shop,

---

1 I am quoting Montaigne from M.A. Screech's translation (Penguin Classics 1991) in comparison with the Pléiade-edition of *Œuvres Complètes* edited by Albert Thibaudet & Maurice Rat (1962). Reference is given in the text as part, chapter, English page, French page. Here: I: 39, 271, 236.

keeping it entirely free and establishing there our true liberty, our principal solitude and asylum." (I: 39, 270, 235) In this asylum he is about to involve himself in the kind of writing that 20 years, 3 volumes and 107 chapters later, will be called *essay*.

Montaigne withdraws and he starts to write. What made him withdraw? What made him start reflecting on himself in the form that was to be called "essay"? Why did Michel, *sieur de* Montaigne, a well-established nobleman in the middle of his life, refrain from social obligations, career, court life and other such occupations in order to devote himself to writing; to learned labor (that was hardly becoming a nobleman); to such an unpracticed and unknown entity as *himself*? What made him call this unexpected activity "essay"?

While there are no simple answers to these questions, many possible answers are scattered in the essays and some of them will be discussed here. Let me first underline the originality of Montaigne's endeavor. Withdrawing from worldly business was hardly original (not even for the nobility). The monastery was the well-established address when one felt like withdrawing from the world. Life in the monastery was motivated by religion: withdrawing from the world was a way to God. When Montaigne carves the motto επεζω, *I refrain*, in a beam, the message is not that he wants to give the world up to come closer to God; the message is rather that he wants to refrain from making hasty judgments and in that manner come closer to himself. Introspection and self-scrutiny were well-known phenomena: from the tradition of the oracle in Delphi came the motto *know thy self* – Montaigne likes to quote this — and early in the Middle Ages the church *padre* Augustine scrutinized himself in his *Confessions*. Several Christian mystics had developed introspection into a route of knowledge. The religiously motivated scrutiny is a matter of *getting away* from oneself; instead of this, Montaigne's version was *approaching* oneself by *constructing* oneself in writing.

Montaigne was original in calling this enterprise *essay*. The word itself was of course in use — it goes back to *exagium* from Middle Age Latin, and has to do with "measure" and "scale" (the word is related to the Classic *examen*). In Montaigne's day, *essay* meant something along the lines of test or sample. The word could be used as a verb, meaning examine, testing. When Montaigne started writing he used *essay* mostly as an active verb describing his searching and examining writing. Following a period of essayistic activity, he starts including the result in the word. "Essay" connects his writing activity with the experiences made during writing: an essay is an activity as well as a result. During his lifetime the essays were published as *Essais* – indefinite form for "essay" and "experience" — but in the first edition after his death they are already called in the definite form *Les Essais, The Essays*. That was the birth of the genre *essay*.

Perhaps Montaigne got his essayistic ideas from consulting books and pondering the 57 inscriptions that were carved on the beams; most of these turn up now and again in the essays. (It may of course have been the other way around: the inscriptions made after the essays). Some of them, for example *All is Vanity*, are derived from what seems to be Montaigne's favorite passage in the Bible: *Ecclesiastes*. Almost all of them come from "classical" literature, as does Montaigne's library and his reading. From Terence, he took a well-known motto: *I am a human and nothing human is alien to me*. Perhaps Montaigne found some comfort when pondering this phrase from Sophocles: *The sweetest life is to think about nothing at all*. Many maxims come from Sextus Empiricus, a Greek astronomer, physician and philosopher from the third century AD; his *Outlines of Pyrrhonism* is a gathering of important contributions to skeptical philosophy. From Sextus Empiricus come laconic mottos that invite speculation. For instance: *I investigate. I do not understand. I decide nothing*. At slightly greater length: *No human being has ever known anything for sure, nobody will ever know anything for sure*. A summary of skeptical logic follows: *Against every statement there can be made another statement of equal validity*. My favorite is already quoted: επεζω, meaning "I refrain," meaning "I refrain from drawing conclusions" or from passing sentence. It is not difficult to understand that this made sense for Montaigne, who had withdrawn from his career as a lawyer, who had voluntarily refrained from passing sentence: not only a logical restraint but also a moral retreat. Not only a retreat: Montaigne withdraws to his tower and his library where something new is emerging. This novelty is the essay and together with the essay, the construction of a new self.

The most famous of Montaigne's mottos he formulated personally and had engraved on a medal: *Que sçay-je?* – "What do I know?" It is just as open and ambiguous as any of the cryptic sentences derived from Sextus Empiricus and it could be understood to be a resigned shrug as well as unprejudiced curiosity. The motto stands as a text under a scale and we remember that the scale is affiliated with the word "essay". I prefer thinking of *Que sçay-je?* as an announcement of sincerity and susceptibility, a usable motto for the essayistic endeavor therefore. This is, above all, an open, testing and inquisitive way of writing, allowing Montaigne to write about anything. "I take the first subject Fortune offers: all are equally good for me." (I: 50, 337, 289) He writes about thumbs, coaches, cannibals, books … about loneliness, idleness, vanity, knowledge and experience. If you manage to follow him you can be sure to find yourself treading a winding road scattered with digressions, whims, contradictions. His way of writing is well described in one of the early essays: "On Idleness" (Part I, chapter 8). In a description of what happened when he withdrew to his tower, he also fixates the birth of the essay:

> Recently I retired to my estates, determined to devote myself as far as I could to spending what little life I have left quietly and privately; it seemed to me then that the greatest favor I could do for my mind was to leave it in total idleness, caring for itself, concerned only with itself, calmly thinking of itself. I hoped it could do that more easily from then on, since with the passage of time it had grown mature and put on weight. But I find – *Variam semper dant otia menis* [Idleness always produces fickle changes of mind] — that on the contrary it bolted off like a runaway horse, taking far more trouble over itself than it ever did over anyone else; it gives birth to so many chimeras and fantastic monstrosities, one after another, without order or fitness, that, so as to contemplate at my ease their oddness and their strangeness, I began to keep a record of them, hoping in time to make my mind ashamed of itself. (I: 8, 31, 34)

Montaigne withdraws to his tower; he sits down amongst his books with the purpose of having no purpose and doing nothing at all. At the same moment, something happens to his mind, his *esprit*: it runs away in an unexpected and unintended activity. This activity is Montaigne starting to *make essay*. The comparison between the mind and the horse, both on the run, is striking — not least since it comes from the horseman Montaigne, who could spend days on end on horseback. According to one of his best followers from the 19th century, Ralph Waldo Emerson, "we cannot afford to take the horse out of Montaigne's essays."[2] In this case, it is tempting to imagine the runaway horse as a version of the horse used by the Classic poet for divine inspiration: *Pegasus*. But Montaigne's horse is not a Greek horse: it is not governed by any divine powers, only by himself. Not this even: his mind-horse is on the run, meaning that it runs freely, meaning that it is wild, out of hand, out of control. It creates "chimeras" and "monstrosities" without

---

2 *Journal* IX, New York 1909–14, p. 152.

"order". Montaigne uses strong words to make it clear that he is writing without purpose, without plan, without model — and in a highly characteristic gesture, he belittles the essayistic activity that he is using all his energy to develop. You could also interpret his pretending as an unassuming position, as an effort to become "Socratic": Montaigne's withdrawal means that he sees through the world and sees through himself, knowing that he knows nothing.

Montaigne's withdrawal does not lead to a quiet life, not to the serenity the skeptics called *ataraxia*. His withdrawal is strategic: he seeks out the spot where he can gather his powers to develop that galloping activity symbolized by the runaway horse. The result is called essay and Montaigne outlines the aesthetics of the essay here with terms that point to the unpredictable and the boundless. Earlier in the same chapter, he talks about the "madness" and "raving lunacy" produced by the erring mind. The French terms "folie" and "rêverie" reappear often when Montaigne wishes to characterize his own writing – and he frequently wants to do exactly that. Montaigne chooses terms that have no place in classical poetics. He wants us to know that his essays cannot be read and judged according to traditional norms; he writes, so to speak, without really writing. "Folie" and "rêverie": the words implicate that the essayistic text lacks structure but is structuring itself. The essay neglects the models for writing that were taught by the discipline of rhetoric; the essays roam just as freely as the runaway horse. When Montaigne calls the result a "chimera", he seems to say that it is inconstant and transitory. When he calls it a "monstrosity", he says that it is put together by contradictory pieces, that it defies nature – implying that it is transgressing the literary system that was considered natural.

The monster-metaphor has followed the essay ever since its invention by Montaigne: the essay shows affinities to many literary genres without fitting in. The essay is subjective and self-promoting without being autobiographical; it can be lyrical without being poetry. Plato had already talked about "the old quarrel" between philosophy and literature and in this "quarrel" the essay takes an intermediary position: it is literary without being fictitious, philosophical without making conceptual analysis. It carries the characteristics of the philosophical dialogue but still it has no dialogue. Every effort to classify the essay ends up negatively: the essay is just as cursory and difficult to delimit as a *chimera* and just as unnaturally put together as a *monster*.

Idle prose

The comparison between the mind and the runaway horse comes in the chapter devoted to "idleness," *oisiveté*. It is one of Montaigne's favorite terms and it could also be translated as passivity or indolence. The word is, of course, related to the Latin *otium*, referring to the free time devoted to contemplation by Renaissance humanists. In the final chapter of book II, "On the resemblance of children to their fathers", the word is again associated with essayistic writing: "All the various pieces of this faggot are being bundled together on the understanding that I am only to set my hand to it in my own home and when I am oppressed by too lax an idleness." (II: 37, 858, 736) As you can see idleness, along with writing, is restricted to the tower ("my own home") and idleness consequently *forces* him to write . In a later chapter, "On vanity" from book III, the term comes up again. In the beginning of the chapter, Montaigne complains about the corruption and misery of his time. Nobody is spared and everyone contributes, some with evil design, "the weaker ones like me contribute silliness, vanity and idleness." (III:9, 1071, 923) With his usual ambiguity, he has named three of his favorite themes: "silliness" (*sottise*) has to do with the insight that you know nothing. "Vanity" has to do with the change and inconstancy of existence. "Idleness" has to do with essayistic writing. Later on in the same chapter, Montaigne returns to his idleness: it is the reason, he writes, that he "renounces" his participation in the world. Instead he is "content to enjoy the world without being over-occupied with it" (III: 9, 1078, 930). He keeps saying that *idleness* and *candor* (*oisiveté, franchise*) are his foremost qualities, meaning that he is not dependent on others and is without obligations.

As we can see, idleness is related to the withdrawal into private life. You may imagine Montaigne as an Epicurean with anarchistic inclinations, living *on* the world instead of *in* the world. I therefore hasten to emphasize that Montaigne's idleness has nothing to do with irresponsibility and that his famous tower is no monastery. The idleness of the tower is all about perspective and self-reflection. In order to acquire perspective, you have to find a spot beside or above your own normality: that is the tower, Montaigne's *arrière-boutique*. To reflect on your own and other people's idle doings you have to aim for idleness.

Montaigne's idleness moves between action and reaction, activity and passivity. The first step towards the essay is a kind of passivity: a withdrawal from public life. It is a kind of *active passivity*: Montaigne does not have to quit, he *resigns* from his office, he is not sent to the tower but uses his free will and designs his essayistic sanctuary with striking energy and enthusiasm. That is not to say that he planned that his passive endeavor, his idleness, would result in the essay. Instead, the impression imparted is that his essayistic activity in the tower was the result of being aimlessly open: again a kind of passivity. If the first phase of idleness is *active passivity*, then the second phase, the phase of writing, is *passive activity*. Both terms are equally important: during the years that he voluntarily enters idle passivity, Montaigne develops his magnificent essayistic activity resulting in three volumes of essays and the genre Essay as an unexpected bonus. Still, this eruptive essayistic activity is passive in the sense that Montaigne never submits to any given poetics or final purpose. The beginnings of the essays is unclear and they have no obvious purpose. The project involved in the essayistic writing seems to be the writing itself. This also means that Montaigne passively follows each and every fancy during his writing. He is unwilling to finish his manuscript but prefers to add and embellish. "I make additions but not corrections" (III: 9, 1091, 941), he claims in the chapter "On vanity," an essay that includes an extensive discussion of his essayistic poetics. He is of course exaggerating: he corrected quite a lot, but still more was added. In the edition from 1588 he had written much in the margins of the manuscript to the first two books (besides writing the essays of the third book) and he continues to add in the margins of his own printed copy. This has bequeathed the philologists a rich selection of textual levels to manage. And it strikes me as an important contribution to the aesthetics of prose. The addition, the filling out of the margins, is a strategy for establishing consistency, coherence, continuity, avoiding gaps and breaks, for making prose.

I have presented Montaigne's "idleness" as an important component in his essayistic endeavor. Idleness moves between action and reaction, activity and passivity. *Movement* is indeed a characteristic of Montaigne's writing. In the chapter "On vanity", Montaigne associates idleness with "vagabonds and loafers" (*vagabons et faineants*) (III:9, 1071, 923): passive but freely roaming characters, not unlike the runaway horse. These characters are worthy of blame since they are idle and irresponsible. But they are also praiseworthy: owing to their mobility (= activity) they prefigure the freedom of man and the inscrutable laws of existence. Further on in the same chapter these dubious *vagabons* turn up again. Montaigne is praising Plato's dialogues, their "motley of ideas," their "jumps and tumblings." And it is the same with his own writing: his "pen" — his *style* — "and his mind both go a-roaming," *vont vagabondant*. (III: 9, 1125, 973)

The writing of essays is therefore a movable, roaming, unbound and irresponsible activity conditioned by idleness. The word *vagabon* has to do with *vagare* (Medieval Latin) and is therefore related to *reexvagare*, a word that in French developed into *rêverie*. At the beginning, the word meant wandering about and in the old days simply referred to mental derangement. Montaigne is probably the first to give the word a literary dimension, although ambiguously; like his idle vagabonds (and a great deal else) it is both positive and negative. The chapter "On educating children" in Book I starts with Montaigne disparaging his writing by describing it as roaming dreams: "I can see – better than anyone else – that all these writings of mine are no more than the ravings of a man who has never done more than taste the outer crust of knowledge." These "ravings" — *resveries* — are further characterized when Montaigne writes that my "concepts and judgment can only fumble their way forward, swaying, stumbling, tripping over." (I: 26, 164f. 144f.) "Judgment" [*jugement*] has legal implications and we remember that the ex-lawyer Montaigne has refrained from passing judgment in order to write his essays. Calling his capacity for judgment fumbling and "stumbling" — *mon jugement ne marche qu'à tastons* – is another version of his suspension of judgment: the "fumbling" (*à tâtons*) is a term that returns when Montaigne describes his essayistic writing. The "fumbling" indicates its lack of planning, its lack of logical disposition and clear-cut conclusions. "Even in the case of my own writings I cannot always recover the flavor of my original meaning" — thus Montaigne states in a later chapter — "I go backwards and forwards: my judgment does not always march straight ahead, but floats and bobs around." (II: 12, 637, 549)

Montaigne's essays are indeed cluttered with descriptions of his essayistic practice — he is what we might call a self-conscious writer although he could not know what he was up to when he started writing. The terms used are often depreciating and always ambiguous: he uses words that oscillate between a positive and a negative meaning, like *vagabond, rêverie, à tâtons*. Another word with the same characteristics is *forgetfulness*, often used by Montaigne in order to describe his inability to be a public servant and a systematic writer as well as his lack of ambition and vindictiveness: "I am so outstanding a forgetter that, along with all the rest, I forget even my own work and writings." (II: 17, 740, 635) Montaigne forgets his obligations as a man of family and nobility; at least he forgets them when he enters his tower. He also forgets the rules established by rhetoric governing all writing; he wants to give us the impression that he writes whatever comes to mind. Forgetfulness is his negative strategy to suspend judgment and refrain from rules and normality. Forgetfulness and idleness are the qualities that accompany the withdrawal to the tower. In the tower, the same qualities are positive tools for liberating discoveries. We have to be grateful for all this forgetting and idling that made it possible for Montaigne's mind to run away from all established forms of writing in order to write his essays and create a genre: the Essay.

The Self

Jean Starobinski is, to my knowledge, the modern critic that best displays the wavering mobility that characterizes Montaigne's essays. In his great book *Montaigne en Mouvement* (*Montaigne in Action* 1982) he points out that Montaigne's withdrawal to the tower can be regarded as a founding act and as a drawing of the boundary between the observing, reflecting essayistic self — and the observed world and observed self. The reason for the withdrawal is that Montaigne wants to define himself in a solid and coherent way. And the reason for this is that he is fed up with the world of dissimulation, hypocrisy and permanent change. But the essayistic movement is not restricted to the withdrawal. This is only the first step in an intense traffic between observation and participation. Montaigne starts his project in order to reach stability but the result is a new concept of human identity as changing and mobile. He withdraws from the falseness of the world and the human masquerade. But the new man that he finds and defines in his essayistic endeavor is just as disguised and constructed as the one he left behind, the only difference is that he is aware of this: "I think that I am an ordinary sort of man, except in considering myself to be one." (II: 17, 722, 618)

In this rapid summary of Starobinski's argument, I have emphasized a purpose with the essayistic activity: *the self*. Starobinski insists that Montaigne is involved in a project concerning identity. This is no simple project because the self is doubled up into a reflecting self and an observed self: Montaigne in his tower scrutinizes himself outside the tower. The double and self-reflecting self is an unstable and mobile self that many have associated with a modern and problematic identity; this is, no doubt, an anachronistic way of modernizing a 16th century French nobleman from the provinces. Still, we cannot shut our eyes to the fact that Montaigne took an intense interest in the construction of his writing identity. "I am myself the subject of my book" — that is how he puts it, as early as in the foreword "To the reader." And in the very last chapter from book III: "I study myself more than any other subject, that is my metaphysics; that is my physics." (III: 13, 1217, 1050) Montaigne is a pioneer of *life writing* – a topic I shall discuss in chapter 7 – and this autobiographical impulse is closely connected with his invention of an essayistic way of writing.

Perhaps Montaigne started out with the ambition of "painting" a self-portrait for the benefit of his friends and his family. He often uses the term "paint" in his many descriptions of himself but he soon realized that it cannot be a "definite" portrait: the object, Montaigne himself, is too unstable and mobile. "The brush-strokes of my portrait do not go awry even though they change and vary". Thus Montaigne in the chapter "On repenting" from book III. He goes on to explain that it is the movable and ever changing conditions of existence which make him write and that the same conditions infect the portrait of himself: "If my soul could only find a footing I would not be assaying myself [*m'essaierois*] but resolving myself. But my soul is ever in its apprenticeship and being tested." (III:2, 907f, 782)

If we imagine Montaigne as making a self-portrait in the style of the Renaissance painters, we have to add that the picture becomes complicated owing to his self-conscious reflections on his art. We do not only read a portrait by someone who "paints" himself, but a portrait of someone painting a painter that paints himself. As a comparison from the visual arts we can think of Velasquez' famous *Las Meninas* (1656) where a complicated twist of perspective makes us see the artist in action while the artist seems to look at us as well as the royal family that he is portraying. This points out the artistic activity: we cannot isolate the portrait from the making of the portrait. Montaigne formulates a similar predicament in the chapter "On giving the lie" in Book II:

> Even if nobody reads me, have I wasted my time when I have entertained myself during so many idle hours with thoughts so useful and agreeable? Since I was modeling this portrait on myself, it was so often necessary to prepare myself and to pose so as to draw out the detail that the original has acquired more definition and has to some extent shaped itself. By portraying myself for others I have portrayed my own self within me in clearer colors than I possessed at first. *I have not made my book any more than it has made me — a book of one substance with its author*, proper to me and a limb of my life; (II: 18, 755, 648.)[3]

This passage is one of the late additions that Montaigne wrote in the margin of his copy of the edition from 1588. He invites us to read it as a summary of his experiences when writing about himself. Or rather: *writing himself*. The lines that I have italicized in the quoted passage seem to emphasize that the self is so involved with the writing that self and writing are "of one substance" — the French word is that the book is *consubstantiel* with its writer. This remarkable expression indicates that the self and the writing must be understood as mutually dependent, the self as a result of writing and the writing being a result of the activities of the self. The passage also shows that Montaigne has been "portraying" [*peignant*] himself in "colors" that are "clearer" than in reality – and that real Montaigne then had to adjust according to written Montaigne.

A little later Montaigne writes, "I listen to my dreams [*reveries*] since I have to enlist [*enroller*] them." (ibid. Transl. modified). This little phrase demonstrates the complications of Montaigne's life writing: there is an idle, dreaming self as well as a listening and actively writing ("enlisting") self. The writing self seems to be in command and the listener has to adjust to the writer. Still, these selves are mutually dependent and basically the same: "of one substance." There are many similar descriptions of the consequences of self-reflection and life writing. Here is a late addition to an early essay: "I discover myself more by accident than by the inquiring of my judgment." (I: 10, 40, 41 transl. modified) Here is a late chapter:

---

3   For some reason Screech has dropped the final clause of the sentence quoted: "non d'une occupation et fin tierce et estrangere comme tous autres livres." ["not of an occupation and end that is beyond and strange like all other books."]

"I realize that there is an unexpected benefit from this publication of my manners: in some ways it serves me as a rule. Occasionally the thought presents itself to me that I should not prove disloyal to this account of my life." (III: 9, 1108, 958)

Montaigne's discovery — his being "of one substance" with his writing — has surprising consequences. One is that he *constructs* himself in writing, making a distinction between a living and "dreaming" self, an observing and "listening" self and then the written self. The living self has to listen to the written self and even adjust to it. Instead of stabilizing the written self, his self-reflection facilitates the discovery of the plurality of the self. Montaigne is calling attention to this consequence when in the final chapter of book III, he writes: "I who make no other profession but getting to know myself find in me such boundless depths and variety that my apprenticeship bears no other fruit than to make me know how much there remains to learn." (III: 13, 1220, 1052) The "apprenticeship": the process of writing from the moment that Montaigne withdrew to the tower and up to his last addition. What he has learnt: that the writing construction of the self is the discovery of the "boundless depths" of the self.

This discovery may well come as no surprise for us, living in a time after Freud for example. But in Montaigne's day I am tempted to call it epochal. It is not only a discovery of the "depth" of the self but also of its plurality and the essays are rich in examples on the variety and plurality of the self. In the chapter, "On the inconstancy of our actions" we read: "We are entirely made up of bits and pieces, woven together so diversely and shapelessly that each one of them pulls its own way at every moment. And there is as much difference between us and ourselves as there is between us and other people." (II: 1, 380, 321) The French word for "bits and pieces" is *lopins*, it could also be translated as "patches" and normally refers to a piece of land in a field cultivated with many different crops. There are further metaphorical possibilities in the quotation. When "bits and pieces" are said to be "woven together", the French equivalent is *contexture*, in this setting this means something like "text" or even "structure". That "we" can be regarded as walking textual structures must have been a striking thought for this writer, who actively tried to construct himself by transforming a medley of literary impressions and quotations into an experience and a text of his own.

Montaigne is employing drastic metaphors to say that the self is just as manifold as the world, that the "bits and pieces" of the self have their own individual projects and these are not necessarily harmonized. Montaigne often states that you and we are different and he always pleads respect for difference. Here he is celebrating difference by saying that my self consists of several selves, all different.

This idea returns in several versions. In the chapter just quoted we read that, "even sound authors are wrong in stubbornly trying to weave us into one invariable and solid fabric." (II:1, 373, 315) Again, it is *contexture* that has been translated as "fabric". Montaigne prefers a writer who would "judge a man in his detail, piece by piece, separately" — he wants the writer to recognize the difference that is already there. Montaigne considers *distinguo*, "I make difference," to be his prime method for describing a reality that is put together in pieces, *pieces rapportées*. Another version of the same expression turns up in a later chapter, accompanied by the following colorful statement: "Man, totally and throughout, is but patches and many-coloured oddments", *rapiessement et bigarrure*. (II: 20, 766, 656).

Montaigne can imagine his own portrait as it is given in the essays, as a *skeletos*, an anatomy, but also as a patchwork, meaning that veins and muscles are woven together in a *contexture*, but that every component lives its own life and that the part is more important than the whole. *If* there is something like a whole – Montaigne invites us to think of the part as primary and the whole as fluctuating and secondary. The different parts of the self can be distinguished by the eye but they are also temporally separated, provided we trust the concept of the patchwork being not only a *contexture* of pieces but also of "moments", that all play their own games.

Of course it is sequences like these that have tempted contemporary readers to associate the plural personality of Montaigne with "post modernity" — although "pre modern" is probably a more accurate term for a French country gentleman at the end of the 16th century. I find the value of such labels doubtful and prefer thinking that Montaigne is trying to express an experience that anyone can have (regardless of any difference historic conditions might make). Let us call it an experience of the manifold self — together with the suspicion that the components of the self are not always adequately coordinated. In the chapter where he describes himself as in "bits and pieces", he also writes that "every sort of contradiction can be found in me, ... timid, insolent; chaste, lecherous; talkative, taciturn;

tough, sickly; clever, dull; brooding, affable; lying, truthful; learned, ignorant; generous, miserly and then prodigal." (II: 1, 377, 319). Montaigne not only finds these distinctions within himself, but he means that "anyone who studies himself attentively finds in himself and in his very judgment this whirring about and this discordancy." The different parts of the self each live out individual lives but they also interrelate and interact, making the self into a contradictory whole (if you can talk about a whole).

Montaigne's diagnosis is certainly not an attack on this plurality, which he registers rather with a resignation that at times transforms into enthusiasm. He can for instance become polemic against the epicurean idea that pain should be diminished making life uniform and affording more space for pleasure. "Truly", Montaigne declares, "anyone who could uproot all knowledge of pain would equally eradicate all knowledge of pleasure and finally destroy Man." (II: 12, 549, 473) The assertion that man is a patchwork of "bits and pieces" is so fundamental that efforts to eliminate or diminish contrasts and contradictions must therefore be regarded as against humanity. Pain/pleasure is still not the decisive contradiction for Montaigne's essayistic experience, nor are any of the other contrasts that he lists. Rather, the experience is associated with plurality in itself and the experience of manifold self is intimately related to the writing project. With stubborn consequence, Montaigne constructs a text based upon the experience of contradiction and plurality; that text is the essay. The autobiographer normally presents a homogenous version of the self that follows a predictable development; Montaigne, on the other hand, offers his patchwork and leaves harmonizing up to the reader. It is tempting to employ an overused metaphor here and say that we meet Montaigne as "text" or, in his own terminology, as *contexture*. Whether or not we opt for plurality or the whole in this rich fabric depends on both our capacity and wishes. The essayistic world is, in any case, a function of the plurality that Montaigne finds in himself and in the world. The essayistic project — the aesthetics of the essay — is an immense effort to preserve this contradictory plurality in writing.

Solitude, skepticism

The chapter "On solitude" in the first book provides interesting clues to the aesthetics and ethics of Montaigne's essayistic prose. Although it is an early chapter it is covered with late additions, indicating that Montaigne returned often to the problematic outlined here.

The chapter introduces a conflict between a life in action and a life in solitude (although Montaigne admits the possibility that this is only an apparent conflict). He insists that solitude is necessary. You should "if possible" have a family, property and good health but you should not depend on these lifelines for an active life. Instead, you should "set aside a room" for yourself: an *arrière-boutique*, according to the phrase I quoted at the outset of this chapter. (I: 39, 270, 235) When Montaigne declares that he has "lived quite enough for others" and wants to devote the remainder of his life to himself, it is difficult to avoid the impression that he is mounting a defense for his essayistic project. His term for the "remainder of his life" (also quoted earlier) — *ce bout de vie* — is interesting. In a later chapter from book III, he uses the same word, *bout*, in order to describe death as the final phase of life (and not as its goal, *but*). (III: 12, 1191, 1028) The "remainder" of life is the time of solitude and it is close to death, but it is also the moment of the essay: it is the free time between life and death, creating the space that is necessary for distance and self-reflection.

Directly following on from this appeal to the "remainder" of life, Montaigne has added a section developing his argument and transforming the possibility of solitude to something resembling a duty: "It is time to slip our knots with society now that we can contribute nothing to it. /---/ Our powers are failing: let us draw them in and keep them within ourselves." (I: 39, 272, 236) This addition was written perhaps 20 years after the first version and the connection between solitude and old age has thus been strengthened. Moreover perhaps we can discern a touch of pathos? A few pages further on, another addition appears that sets pathos within parentheses and seems to scorn the very project concerning voluntary solitude. Montaigne is now saying that people talking about "withdrawing from the world" are victims of a "ridiculous contradiction": either you are within life or you are leaving it once and for all. Only the religious ascetic is credible when it comes to leaving life. The ascetic aims for "another life, blessedly immortal", but normal people have no reason at all to give up life. (I: 39, 275, 239)

The polemic starts out as a commentary to a few phrases from Pliny and Cicero and the chapter ends with the wisdom of these celebrities being scorned as "verbiage and show". There is certainly an element of critical self-reflection here! Montaigne has devoted the whole chapter to praising the solitude that comes at the "remainder" of life. He has encouraged himself and others to withdraw, with his tower as its symbol. Solitude, along with forgetting and idleness, are conditions for the essayistic project. However, all conditions are ambiguous: idleness becomes the runaway horse of essayistic industry and solitude is never absolute. The literary activity does not provide relief from any worldly trouble and refraining takes us out of the frying pan and into the fire.

This argument is not only a version of Montaigne's self-reflection, but it also seems to be taking a stand for life, including that "remainder" that he wanted to enjoy in solitude. Only the holy man, having God as his objective, can withdraw from this world expecting to find another world. Conversely, the essayist has himself as his objective and it does not matter how tired, old, forgetful and idle he is: he does not refrain from life. It seems as though Montaigne, with his late additions, wishes to remind himself and us that the withdrawal to the tower is merely the first step in the newly written life of the essayist. The addition might even *illustrate* this *second* step: the sudden activity of the unexpected contradiction. It certainly makes the essayistic *rhythm* explicit since it ends by invalidating the contradiction between action and solitude that formed the starting point. The reader *should* be at a loss after having read this essay. The reader should be invited to think that their knowledge is limited, that they actually know nothing. The "remainder" of life is the site for this combination of shortage and profusion.

Montaigne's ambiguous praise of solitude is a variation on a general theme in the essays: his skepticism. A skeptic impulse is already involved in the instituting gesture of the essayistic project: the withdrawal to the tower. With this retreat, Montaigne tries to establish something solid in a world where nothing is stable, neither himself nor his knowledge. "We grasp at everything but clasp nothing but wind" according to one of his many statements of epistemological resignation. (I: 31, 229, 200) Just as his withdrawal triggers his essayistic activity, the skeptic impulse paves the way for his inquisitive excursions into the outside world. The statement just quoted which comments on our futile grasping at everything appears in "On the Cannibals," a chapter that is famous due to Montaigne's interest in those "barbarians" that had been "discovered" in Brazil. He transforms this interest into a severe critique of the Eurocentric view of the world and of the cruelty of the European explorers. His epistemological skepticism — we only clasp "wind", when seeking secure knowledge — is, in other words, part of an argument, where Montaigne develops a critical observation of contemporary events. His skeptical interest in the winds of knowledge and the vanity of the world is not purely a philosophical concern, should there be such a thing. Besides being an important component in the essayistic project, Montaigne's skepticism is integrated in a political argument, allowing him to criticize all possible versions of fundamentalism and Eurocentric cruelty. His aesthetics is always an ethic, often with political implications.

Montaigne lived in an epoch where the views of the world were dramatically altered in their geographical, anthropological and economical structures. These changes provoked the curiosity and confirmed the skepticism of the essayist. In the very first chapter of the first book, he states that "Man is indeed an object miraculously vain, various and wavering." (I: 1, 5, 13). The first chapter of the second book is called "On the inconstancy of our actions" and he starts the following chapter by stating that "The world is all variation and dissimilarity." (II: 2, 381, 321) In the chapter "On coaches" from the third book, Montaigne combines a devastating critique of Spanish actions in Peru and Mexico with equally drastic versions of the changing plurality of the world. If there is a development within the essays in these matters, it is towards a more radical "relativism" and "skepticism" — although I hesitate to use these terms since they can be associated with distance and indifference today. Montaigne's skepticism is nothing of the sort; it is part of his humanitarian profile, his open-mindedness, his pathos of tolerance.

Earlier, I quoted a passage from the chapter "On repenting" in book III, where Montaigne meditates on the fact that his writing a self-portrait does not lead to the stability that was the justification. The portrait is no exception to the law of change: "The brushstrokes of my portrait do not go awry even though they change and vary." (III: 2, 907, 782). He expands this inconstancy into a metaphor for nothing less than existence itself: "The world is but a perennial seesaw", *une branloire perenne*, and if we imagine something as being stable it is only because the seesaw moves slowly. The object of the portrait — himself — is in a state of "natural drunkenness," that is in permanent change, but then his intention with the self-portrait is not to portray "being," *l'estre*, but "becoming," *le passage*. Not any specific and changing passage, but all passages and becoming as such.

Montaigne starts this chapter by referring to his essays as a self-portrait and he returns to the essayistic project after his anti-metaphysical statement. He also indicates that, if only being had been different, if it could show stability and substance, then the essays would be superfluous, the portrait would not "change and vary" but would stabilize. He has also told us that being and reality has no substance and is perennially on the move: thus Montaigne must continue to describe and "assay" himself by writing his essays. There is, of course, nothing remarkable in the observation that Montaigne's essays are based on an epistemological skepticism, nor in the relation between his skepticism and his aesthetics. However it is remarkable that this relation gives him a foundation for critique of human stupidity, vanity and cruelty. The insight that shows everything to be unstable is the stable basis for Montaigne's critical activity and his pathos of tolerance.

Montaigne's ethic can be approached through his theology. In his early years, Montaigne translated the Latin work *Theologia Naturalis* into French and he later devoted his longest and most ambitious essay, "An apology for Raymond Sebond" in the second book, to a discussion of this work. This includes his most extensive epistemological interrogation into skepticism, systematic doubt and *docta ignorantia*, that is, his idea of ignorance as the most reliable knowledge. In this very ambiguous "apology," he devotes hundreds of pages to all possible versions of skepticism and he reaches the conclusion that his own ignorance is no private whim. His skepticism seems to be rooted in the very structure of being: "there is no permanent existence either in our being or in that of objects. We ourselves, our faculty of judgment and all mortal things are flowing and rolling ceaselessly: nothing certain can be established about one from the other, since both judged and judging are ever shifting and changing." (II: 12, 680, 586)

The final word in this quotation ("changing"), is a translation of the French *branle*, a meaning that we meet again in Montaigne's *branloire perenne*, the eternal seesaw, situated at the very center of existence. There are many possible reactions to the predicament that he expresses with his skepticism concentrated in this metaphor, for instance religious belief or silence. However the essayist's reaction is neither to take the leap into faith, nor to observe a skeptical silence. On the contrary, it is to get moving and the movement of the essayist lies in writing. The first obligation for the essayist is simply: keep writing![4] Only by writing Montaigne can construct the new, movable and modern self so to speak. By writing, he shows that the unreliable and permanently changing reality is the only reality worth writing about. The changing impressions of the senses may restrict or even invalidate human knowledge, but the kingdom of the senses is nevertheless the homeland of the essays and the essayistically constructed (and constructing) human being.

Keep writing! Such is the core of the essayistic project and such is Montaigne's contribution to the aesthetics of prose. The essayistic homeland is a prosaic world of permanent change. This world can only be described and expressed in a prose with the same characteristics: A feeble beginning. No end. No finality. A permanent flow of additions.

---

4   I am using an observation by John Snyder, *Prospects of Power. Tragedy, Satire, the Essay and the Theory of Genre*. Kentucky UO 1991, p. 152.

Nietzsche: Performative Prose

Is Nietzsche writing philosophy or literature or both? This question is often posed yet is difficult to answer. Nevertheless, we should keep asking the question in order to approach Nietzsche's handling of the old strife between philosophy and literature. According to a well-known phrase, "style equals man". Moreover, according to a well-known Nietzschean maxim, man is "the animal *whose nature has not yet been fixed.*"[5] Following on from this, I like to think of Nietzsche's style of prose as not yet determined, his writing as undefined, unfinished and undecided. Nietzsche writes the impossible! The *impossibility* of a clear-cut definition has to do with Nietzsche's experimental style and his various efforts to imbue his prose with a *performative* dimension. Nietzsche is always on the move and this makes him an exemplary contributor to the aesthetics of prose: prose as a continuous effort to make thinking, experience, life, continuous – while allowing for contingency and mobility. I will present this version of Nietzsche in three sections: first, some efforts to characterize his writing in relation to the idea of a finished *work*; then his philosophy of *style*; and finally, his fondling of indeterminate words like *perhaps* and *or*.

Aphoristic work

Nietzsche often discusses his own way of writing and he likes to command our reading. An oft-quoted passage appears in the preface to *On the Genealogy of Morality* from 1887. Nietzsche tells us that his aphoristic form can present difficulties if the aphorism is not read with due gravity:

---

5 *Beyond Good and Evil*, transl. R.J. Hollingdale, Penguin Classics 1990, p. 88. Reference will be given in the text.

> An aphorism, properly stamped and molded, has not been 'deciphered' just because it has been read out; on the contrary, this is just the beginning of its proper *interpretation*, and for this, an art of interpretation is needed. In the third essay [*Abhandlung*] of this book I have given an example of what I mean by 'interpretation' in such a case: – this treatise [*Abhandlung*] is a commentary on the aphorism that precedes it. I admit that you need one thing above all in order to practice the requisite *art* of reading, a thing which today people have been so good at forgetting – and so it will be some time before my writings are 'readable'-, you almost need to be a cow for this one thing and certainly *not* a 'modern man': it is *rumination* …⁶

Here, Nietzsche actually presents several possibilities for reading his writing. He confirms that he pens *aphorisms*; but not *only* aphorisms. The *Genealogy* contains three *Abhandlungen* and the last demonstrates the art of reading by interpreting an aphorism. Thus, *Genealogy* consists of aphorisms, interpretations and *Abhandlungen*, ordered in short, numbered pieces. The three *Abhandlungen* are preceded by a *Preface* and that is also organized in a series of eight pieces, the last containing the quoted passage concerning the aphorism and the art of reading as a ruminating repetition.

Numbering is indeed Nietzsche's typical device for organizing his aphorisms. Sometimes he prefers to refer to his smallest unit as *Sentenzen*: sententious phrases. In *Human, All Too Human* we find a praise of the *Sentenz* (volume II, nr 168) and, in a note from 1882, where Nietzsche is testing different titles (as he often does), every new title is followed by the subtitle *Sentenzen-Buch*. Or some other test-titles that are not so common: main piece, letters, maxims and arrows. Not to mention all those prefaces and epilogues that Nietzsche uses to wrap up his texts.

The aphorism is probably the best of these terms: it is flexible and it associates Nietzsche with some of his favorite writers: Pascal, Lichtenberg. The aphorism covers compact, insistent and enigmatic pieces of writing from a couple of lines up to a couple of pages: exactly the kind of writing cultivated by Nietzsche from *Human, All Too Human* up to the end of his career. The aphorism should be understood in a wide sense as that which is "secluded, discreet, segmented."⁷ The aphorism in this sense dominates not only

---

6 Transl. Carol Diethe, Cambridge University Press, 1994, p. 9f.
7 I borrow the characteristic from Werner Hamacher, "'Disgregation des Willens'. Nietzsche über Individuum und Individualität." In *Entferntes Verstehen*; Frankfurt: Suhrkamp 1998, p. 147.

Nietzsche's published work but also his notebooks: there are several thousand pages of these and much of it appears aphoristic. Just like the finished books, these are organized in files and "books" and are often numbered.

Still, the aphorism is a controversial term for Nietzsche's commentators as well as for Nietzsche himself. When he names his main sections in *Genealogy Abhandlungen*, he uses the preface already quoted in order to modify this designation: "this *Abhandlung* is a commentary on the aphorism that precedes it" ... Nietzsche's commentators differ in their view of this aphorism – they may locate it to the Truth or the Woman or the whole introductory section.[8] Still, Nietzsche's modification seems to indicate that his *Abhandlung* is not an *Abhandlung* but a *commentary*: a version of that philological activity that makes up the art of interpretation and is called *reading*. This art is characterized, as we recall from the quotation, as inaccessible for "modern man", since it demands a *ruminating*, dwelling and repetitive slowness. The philologist is, according to another preface – in the *Daybreak* – "a teacher of slow reading."[9]

Is Nietzsche revealing himself as a commentator, as a philologist?

The thought is tempting ... and may contain some truth. At least it is true that Nietzsche is interested in the art of reading: he often asks to be closely read; in this respect he is a dialogical writer. This is explicit in *The Case of Wagner* for instance, since it consists of twelve *letters*. But this observation must also be modified. If Nietzsche asks for a dialogue, he asks in a choleric and imperious way. He does not wait for an answer and he prefers addressing a future reader to a contemporary. In this sense he prefers monologue to dialogue and he fills his monologues with enigmatic aphorisms and irrefutable *Sentenzen*. A monologic dialogue! In the *Zarathustra*-books he invents a dialogical situation, with teacher and pupils, and immediately transforms the teacher to a lonely and untouchable prophet ...

These preliminary observations are meant to demonstrate that every determination of Nietzsche's way of writing asks for modifications

---

8 Kelly Oliver (*Womanizing Nietzsche*, NY: Routledge 1995, p. 20) insists (in polemics against Alexander Nehamas, *Nietzsche. Life as Literature*, Harvard UP 1985, p. 114) that Nietzsche has Woman in mind. John T. Wilcox gives a critical summary of the debate in "The Exegesis of an Aphorism in *Genealogie III*: Reflections on the Scholarship". *Nietzsche-Studien* vol. 27, 1998).
9 Transl. R. J. Hollingdale, Cambridge University Press, 1999, p. 5. Reference will be given in the text.

and additions – Nietzsche is cultivating a writing that is not yet determined. And if it is difficult to define *how* he is writing it is just as difficult to answer the question: *what* is he writing? Does he write books? The question may seem ridiculous considering that he published some ten books during his lifetime and that many more have been published in his name after that. But if books are being understood as *works* the question becomes difficult straight away: the question is, whether or not Nietzsche's books are finished *works* and whether one or all of them together may be regarded as a *main work*, a *Hauptwerk*. Alternatively, could all the notebooks that he left behind form the basis of a *main work* that he did not manage to complete?

This question has bothered his commentators, starting with his sister Elisabeth, who took the initiative of compiling different notes into a book that she presented as his *Hauptwerk*: *The Will to Power*. Nietzsche himself seems to have been skeptical of the concept of work, at least regarding the idea of a finished work of art. In the second part of *Human, All Too Human* we find the headline *Against the art of works of art*. The mission of art is to beautify life, according to this passage: "After this great, indeed immense task of art, what is usually termed art, *that of the work of art*, is merely an *appendage*."[10]

This aphorism comes early in Nietzsche's output, around the time when he was dissociating himself from philology and approaching philosophy and literature – after having broken some philological conventions concerning the learned work with *The Birth of the Tragedy*. (Among Nietzsche's books, his book on tragedy comes closest to the idea of a finished "work"). The aphorism quoted seems to side with *life* as the mission of art and thinking and can be understood as if *art* is more important than the *works of art* (the act of thinking being more important than the result; work as activity being more important that the finished work).

The idea of art being in a sense more important than the works of art, transgressing every work of art, is important in the history of aesthetics, not least today. It is also important in Nietzsche's own history, since it contributes to the view of the art of writing as an activity directed to the future with Utopian potentials. Thinking itself should have this Utopian dimension and in that sense transgress the finished works of thought. In the notebooks, that Elisabeth Förster-Nietzsche searched in order to construct *The Will to Power*

---

10 Transl. R.J. Hollingdale, Cambridge University Press 1998, p. 255.

as Nietzsche's main work, his *Hauptwerk*, there are several elements that invite thoughts about Nietzsche's strained relation to the book and the work. A striking element is his recurrent fascination for titles and tables of content. Nietzsche loves to write down ideas to new book titles, often with extensive tables of content. Some of these titles are turned into books but most of them remain abandoned ideas. For example, we would love to read the following works by Nietzsche: *Revaluation of all Values, The Eternal Return, The Great Midday, Midday and Eternity, Towards a History of Modern Gloom, Music, Gai Saber, Sapientia Victrix, The New Enlightenment* ... the last three titles carry the subtitle *Prelude to a Future Philosophy*. This indicates Nietzsche's gesturing to the future: he likes his writing to be regarded as *Prelude*, as reaching into the future (and the formula has survived as a subtitle to *Beyond Good and Evil*).

I have quoted from the notebooks dating from 1885. The *Will to Power* also turns up here, for instance, bearing the subtitle: *Essaying a New Explanation of All that Takes Place*.[11] *Will to Power* returns along with many other titles on several occasions (with various tables of content) and during Spring of 1888 you get the impression that Nietzsche is in fact heading for a philosophical *Hauptwerk* with that title. But that disappears with the last entry of *Will to Power* in August 1888[12] and during the intensely productive last four months of Nietzsche's writing life there are other proposals of titles in other directions and without systematic ambitions.

The thematically presented compilation published by Elisabeth Förster-Nietzsche with the title *Will to Power* has had an immense importance for the reading and reception of Nietzsche. Still, the basis for this in the notebooks is insufficient and it does not fit Nietzsche's view of writing as a process, rather than a finished work. She has, of course, been heavily criticized for the extent of her manipulation of the manuscripts[13] and *Will to Power* is now superceded by the chronological edition of all notes published by Giorgio Colli and Mazzino Montinari in different "critical" editions from 1967, called *Posthumous Fragments*. But even these exemplary philologists permit themselves some freedom with the title. I cannot see that Nietzsche ever uses "fragment" in order to designate what he is writing, neither

---

11 *Kritische Studienausgabe*, Berlin: de Gruyter 1988, vol. 12, p. 19.
12 *Kritische Studienausgabe*, 13: 537.
13 See the commentary in *Kritische Studienausgabe* 14: 383–400 and Mazzino Montinari, *Nietzsche lesen*, Berlin: de Gruyter 1982, p. 92–119.

in notebooks nor in his published work. As we have seen, he tests different terms – aphorism, *Sentenz* and so on – about as often as he comes up with new titles to unwritten books. But the titles are aiming for the future and every proposal of a definite genre is criticized or modified. *Work* and *fragment* do not belong to his vocabulary. Thus we must admit it to be an historical irony that his different publishers have ended up with exactly these terms when publishing what Nietzsche himself did not publish.

Both "work" and "fragment" are heavily invested terms in the history of aesthetics. The work may be called a hermeneutical category, closely related to "totality" and "meaning". The fragment was loaded with aesthetical and philosophical value during German Romanticism. From that time on, the fragment has been understood as a negative counterpart to the positively finished work. Therefore related to modernist attacks against the classical traditions of art and thinking. A neutral description would be that work and fragment are mutually dependant, like extremes on a scale. Nietzsche's ambitions when it comes to "work" go beyond this logic: he exceeds every delimitation of "work" in favor of his ongoing "life-work", an unfinished dialogue (monologue?) displaying his "work" as an enormous amount of "fragments".

Modern French readings of Nietzsche have emphasized the fragmentary character of Nietzsche's writing. According to Gilles Deleuze, in *Nietzsche and Philosophy* (1962), Nietzsche writes aphorisms and he bases his argument on the quotation from *Genealogy* that I cited at the beginning of this chapter. (He seems not to notice that Nietzsche writes that he is *not* writing aphorisms, in *Genealogy*, but *Abhandlungen* containing a "commentary"). The aphorism is in fact a *fragment*, according to Deleuze, meaning that it is "the form of plural thought" relevant for approaching the sense of an existence, an act, a thing. The fragment is above all *not* a *maxim*, since the maxim is closed, definite and singular, while the fragment is open, interpretative and plural, a stylistic version of a subversive, "nomadic" policy.[14]

Nietzsche himself uses neither *fragment* nor *maxim* although he is using *aphorism* (with due modifications). Deleuze's way of handling Nietzsche's text as open and opening (in contrast to traditionally "closed" forms) may be exaggerated. Nevertheless, he identifies something vital in Nietzsche's aesthetics and his thinking: its character of

---

14 Gilles Deleuze, *Nietzsche et la philosophie*, PUF 1962, p. 35f.

a process. It is an unfinished process, perhaps not possible to finish – and his many additions, prefaces and epilogues to everything he published illustrate this process-character just as strikingly as the many titles that are enumerated in his notebooks do.

Jacques Derrida emphasizes this character in *Spurs* (1978). Derrida finds a striking example in one of the notebooks: among hundreds of pages of philosophical speculation from 1881, Nietzsche suddenly writes, "I have forgotten my umbrella."[15] Understanding such a note as a reminder is of course close to hand (although this one is mysteriously written as a quotation and Nietzsche seldom if never uses his notebooks for such reminders). Derrida uses it as a hermeneutical provocation and demonstrates that the fragment (if indeed fragment is the word) can obviously be regarded as pure coincidence beyond all interpretation and meaning – but *also* as a gesture with immense potential for psychosocial and metapoetical meaning. The fragment can be both meaningful and meaningless. This ambivalence and uncertainty may apply to Nietzsche's text in its totality, his groping, undefined and unfinished writing:

> To whatever lengths one might carry a conscientious interpretation, the hypothesis that the totality of Nietzsche's text, in some monstrous way, might well be of the type 'I have forgotten my umbrella' cannot be denied.
> Which is tantamount to saying that there is no totality to Nietzsche's text, not even a fragmentary or aphoristic one.[16]

Derrida's deconstruction excludes every thought of Nietzsche's work as finished *work*. He is also unwilling to use terms such as fragment and aphorism, since these seem to give way to an imaginary totality. Derrida's predecessor, Maurice Blanchot insists, on the other hand, that Nietzsche's writing is *fragmentary*. He is not alluding to the amount of fragments (or aphorisms) but refers instead to a general tendency. In the big chapter, "Nietzsche's fragmentary writing" from *The Infinite Conversation* (1969) Blanchot wants to show that this writing has a pluralistic tendency aiming not at totality or work but at *the absence of the work* – if there is a pathos here, it is a pathos of disappearance. Blanchot regards this fragmentary (or fragmentizing) writing as a version of "crisis". The crisis is historically motivated by the phenomenon Nietzsche called "nihilism", that is the final loss of

---

15 *Kritische Studienausgabe* 9: 587.
16 Transl. Barbara Harlow, Chicago University Press, 1978, p. 133f.

each and every guarantee for values, evaluations and communities. In relation to this historical and metaphysical crisis, Nietzsche's writing is at once a symptom and also the promise of a state beyond values and beyond nihilism. Furthermore, Nietzsche unearths an anthropological insight, a *prima philosophia*, preceding every historical predicament while also denying every idea of an originary unity or totality. According to Blanchot's Nietzsche, it is the fragmentation that is originary. The Dionysian tearing to pieces is the original event, that initiates as well as it ruins all culture: "The first knowledge is knowledge of the tearing apart – the breaking up – of Dionysos."[17]

Blanchot relies on Heidegger's reading of Nietzsche in the sense that he has inherited the idea that Nietzsche's thinking, including the style of his thinking, is a critical answer to a historical predicament: nihilism. Nietzsche expresses this loss of values but he also tries to transgress it. Blanchot and Heidegger draw opposing conclusions from this diagnosis. Blanchot imagines the "work-less" fragmentation as the logical consequence of the crisis; Heidegger imagines the construction of a work, a *Hauptwerk*, as a future possibility and an efficient remedy to handle the nihilistic experience.

It is often said that Heidegger always sided with the Nazis, but this is not quite accurate when it comes to the question of Nietzsche's notebooks. Heidegger is in fact remarkably critical of the compilation published by Elisabeth Förster-Nietzsche as *Will to Power*, a book that had been adopted by Nazi philosophers. This is remarkable because Heidegger was an advisor to the "Nietzsche-Archive", which was responsible for both this publication and also making the notes accessible. (Heidegger left this position in 1942 when a party philosopher was put in charge of the Archive).[18] Heidegger airs his criticism in the lectures on Nietzsche between 1936 and 1946 (published 1960): here he returns to the question of Nietzsche and the work on four occasions, criticizing *Will to Power* because of its anachronistic assembling of notes from different periods under pseudo-systematic headings.[19] This criticism was philosophically (and perhaps politically) motivated.

---

17 Transl. Susan Hanson, Minnesota University Press, 1993, p. 157.
18 More about Heidegger in the Nietzsche-Archive in M. Heinz, Th. Kisiel, "Heideggers Beziehungen zum Nietzsche-Archiv im Dritten Reich". In *Annäherungen an Martin Heidegger*, Frankfurt: Campus Verlag 1996; and in Manfred Riedel, *Nietzsche in Weimar. Ein deutsches Drama*, Leipzig: Reclam 2000, ch. 4.
19 *Nietzsche I-II*, Pfullingen: Neske 1961, I: 18f., I: 411f., I: 481f., II: 43f.

Heidegger regarded Nietzsche's thought as a process or a mode of thought that could not be finished for systematic reasons. Instead, Nietzsche's thought is struck with *krisis* at the very moment when a conclusion approaches. (Heidegger pinpoints this to Nietzsche's final thinking period: 1887–88). Nietzsche's reader must set aside every expectation of a finished work and instead read Nietzsche's text as a mode of thought punctuated with crisis and necessarily unfinished. But the reader must also, at the same time, face the task of developing this mode of thought; ultimately the reader is expected to finish the attempt that Nietzsche started and in that way conquer the nihilism that triggered Nietzsche's *krisis*.

As a result of his view of Nietzsche's writing as a process, Heidegger ignores the differences between Nietzsche's published books and his notebooks. Heidegger also emphasizes that no established concept of text or genre sufficiently designates what Nietzsche writes, at least not his notebook writing. For a lack of useful terminology, Heidegger opts to call the notes "pieces" [*Stücke*]. Heidegger was of course writing at a time when the publication of these *Stücke* was incomplete and unsatisfactory. His wish for chronological accuracy is well fulfilled in the critical editions that are now prevalent. Regardless of this, the crisis-scenario that governs Heidegger's reading has *not* become evident. The view of Nietzsche's writing as a process has dominated my review of commentators and has joined forces with the dominant philology. Still, it has become even more difficult to say something definite about the tendencies and the developments of these writings. My commentators understand Nietzsche's development quite differently, but they all regard the notes – fragments, *Stücke* – as a vital aspect of Nietzsche's writing. They would agree that notes are a different form of expression when compared to finished books, but the boundaries are very loose and the *work* is not an adequate designation of any part.

Nietzsche actually wrote in *three* quite different forms: he wrote his books and his notes but he also penned a great number of *letters*. It is not possible to dismiss any of these three versions of writing as less important than the others. The only failsafe thing to say is that each form of writing takes up an equal proportion of the total volume of Nietzsche's writings. There is no striking development making one form of writing more prominent than the other. There is no tendency of fragmentation. Some of his later books revert to more traditional forms: we have seen that *Genealogy* is organized as

Abhandlungen. The autobiographical *Ecce homo*, written as a book 1888 but never finished by Nietzsche personally, is certainly not fragmentary but clearly organized in four chapters (as usual with a complicated enumeration and presented with an extensive preface). Nietzsche is continuously working with his three forms of expression at the same time. During his last days of writing, in January 1889, he wrote a series of letters *at the same time* as he made notes and *at the same time* as he edited some "dithyrambs" and proofread what was to become the little book, *Nietzsche contra Wagner*.

Nietzsche's three versions of writing – the book, the note, the letter – are his way of developing prose into a form that can cope with the turbulent reality that he is so keen on observing and discussing. His forms relate in a *labyrinthic* manner to each other; similar to the relations between the philosophical *Abhandlung*, the philological commentary and the biographical presentation. The note hides a book, the book hides a letter and the letter hides a note – lines of thought that intersect and then separate, converge and diverge. Meaning that the traditional *work* – the logically organized work – is replaced by one or more labyrinthic forms, without beginning, without centre, without end. Nietzsche's prose is a prose where the *centre is everywhere*, as is self-referentially stated in *Thus spoke Zarathustra*.[20] An open form closing, a closed form opening ... Lines of thought that move apart or in circles ... making up a Nietzsche who is always there and always somewhere else. A frustrating logic beautifully expressed by Nietzsche in a passage from *Twilight of the Idols* when, as usual, he is aiming at something that is not:

> I am the first German to have mastered the aphorism; and aphorisms are the forms of 'eternity'; my ambition is to say in ten sentences what other people say in a book, – what other people do *not* say in a book ...[21]

Style

The Case of Wagner was written in Nietzsche's final, hectic and creative Fall. It gives several hints about Nietzsche's own writing, well hidden behind his violent description of the once admired master.

---
20 *Kritische Studienausgabe* 4: 273.
21 *The Anti-Christ, Ecce Homo, Twilight of the Idols And Other Writings*. Transl. Judith Norman. Cambridge University Press, 2005, p. 223. Reference will be given in the text.

Here, the philological art of reading is united with philosophical analysis and with the biographical information and address of the letter-writer. "Yesterday I heard *Bizet's* masterpiece for – would you believe it? – the twentieth time."[22] Such is the beginning of the first "letter", where Nietzsche profiles *Carmen* against Wagner's collected works with the question of *style* as the recurrent criterion.

In the seventh "letter", where Nietzsche wants to concentrate on "the question of *style*", he characterizes "literary decadence" as:

> The fact that life does not reside in the totality any more. The word becomes sovereign and jumps out of the sentence, the sentence reaches out and blots out the meaning of the page, the page comes to life at the expense of the whole – the whole is not whole any more." (p. 245)

Wagner is his surprising example of a decadent *miniaturist*, whose importance remains "hidden" in his "endless melody". In a postscript to the twelve "letters" Nietzsche asserts that "only small things" can be masterly performed today, only in the detail are integrity and honesty (*Rechtschaffenheit*) possible. (p. 260) One might say that we are halfway between Hegel's "truth is in totality" and Adorno's famous inversion in *Minima Moralia* – see ch. 4 - where "totality" is always a lie. The late Nietzsche seems to lament the loss of totality and the necessity of *Stückwerk,* totality always being "cobbled together, calculated, synthetic, an artifact," as he puts it in the seventh letter. (p. 245) But he can also praise the "small thing" for its *Rechtschaffenheit* and for being magically expressive ("immensely meaningful").

It is tempting to say that Nietzsche is characterizing his own case more than the case of Wagner in this pamphlet. Nietzsche's own style, called "fragmentary" by Blanchot, is well characterized by the words Nietzsche used to describe literary "decadence" (words that he partly borrowed from Paul Bourget). Nietzsche's comparison of Wagner and Bizet also points to Nietzsche himself. In contrast to Wagner's German concept and his "endless sequence", he finds Bizet short and melodious, his orchestral sound is "dry", his passion is Southern and his sensibility is "African" (p. 235). For us – and in contrast to Wagner's nebulous "music drama" – Bizet's *Carmen* comes closer to a "number opera" (even if Nietzsche does not use the term): it consists of a series of loosely connected and well defined scenes and songs, that can be put together and *numbered* – in about the same way as Nietzsche polished and numbered the *Stücke* that he connected for

---

22   Included in the volume quoted in note 21, here p. 234.

his publications. With Nietzsche (as with Bizet), you could say that the totality is put together in an artful and artificial way.

When discussing Bizet, Nietzsche idealized what is, in practice, his own style. When discussing Wagner he is beseeching an ideal that keeps returning. A recurrent term for this ideal is the *grand style* (*grosse Stil*). In the post-script to the Wagner-letters, where Nietzsche pleads for the "small thing" as a reserve for *Rechtschaffenheit*, he also takes the opportunity to criticize the notion of music in "grand style." But only a few months later, in *Ecce homo*, he adds a section on his own *art of style* in the chapter "Why I Write Such Good Books". This book is difficult to evaluate due to its hyperbolic spirit, more so than most of Nietzsche's other books. Here, Nietzsche is hyperbolically characterizing his *Zarathustra*-books: "I was the first to discover the art of *great* rhythm, the *great style* of the period, to express an incredible up and down of sublime, of overmanly passion." (p. 104)

The idea of a "grand style" was just as false in the Wagner-letters (at least in music) as it is superbly true, in *Ecce homo*, as a characteristic of Nietzche's own style. This illustrates that as soon as he comments upon the "grand style", Nietzsche is full of contradictions – he is about as contradictory as when he is discussing Wagner. The term appears for the first time (to my knowledge) in a short notice in *Human, All Too Human*[23], where it is briefly characterized as "beauty" surpassing "the immense" (*das Ungeheure*): as beauty in combination with the sublime. The term keeps coming back in the notebooks and a few times in the finished books. There is never any systematic treatment but there is a note of some length from a later date (Spring 1888):

'Music' – and the grand style

The greatness of an artist has nothing to do with the 'beautiful feelings' that he can arouse: that is for the womenfolk to believe. It has to do with his capacity of approaching the grand style, his power of the grand style. This style has something in common with the great passion: it refrains from pleasing, it forgets to persuade, it commands, it has a *will* ... Becoming master of the chaos that is you; forcing your chaos into form; becoming necessity in form: logical, simple, unambiguous, becoming mathematic, becoming *law* -: such is the grand ambition. ... All the arts know the ambition of the grand style: why is it lacking in music? So far

---

23 *Kritische Studienausgabe* 2: 596.

no musician has built something like the master builder who created Palazzo Pitti?[24]

Wagner looms in the background to these lines. Unlike any other musician in the 19th century, he had strived for music in the grand style. Wagner aimed for music that went beyond music in a dramatic form that went beyond the established form of the drama. And he wrote music that concentrates on "great passion" (at least in Nietzsche's favorite opera from his early years: *Tristan and Isolde*). Unlike any other musician, Wagner tried his hand as a utopian master builder (in Bayreuth). Still, Nietzsche misses the ambition of the grand style in music and he can only think of one example of its realization: the Florentine building *Palazzo Pitti*. This was also the favorite example of the sovereignty of Renaissance culture employed by Nietzsche's admired colleague at Basel, Jacob Burckhardt. The architectonic example returns in *Twilight of the Gods*. Here, Nietzsche imbues the architect with the upper hand in comparison with the actor, the musician and the poet. The justification being that the building can express "the highest feelings of power and self-assurance." The "grand style" does not need to "prove itself", it "scorns to please" and does not wait for an answer (p. 198). The grand style is not seductive or theatrical. It refrains from rhetorical device and it does not use the massive persuasion that the young Nietzsche was seduced by in Wagner's "endless" and emotionally loaded periods. (The same sequences that the bourgeois audience was, to Nietzsche's dismay, willingly seduced by at the newly opened Bayreuth).

In "grand style" you do not persuade or appeal or discuss or play and you do not wait for an answer: you *command*. The reason: you want to reach something unheard of, "form" substituting "chaos", "necessity" substituting the contingency of ordinary reality. The "grand style" reaches for a reality that is *utopian*: a reality that is not yet known. (The Renaissance palace presented as the only known example fits the Renaissance culture well and was very much Burckhardt's utopian construction). The "grand style" is a *music of the future*, to ring the changes on a Wagnerian theme. Nietzsche did not accept Wagner's version but he presented his own style as such futuristic music, as we saw in the quotation from *Ecce homo*.

But: whatever the *grand style* is, it in no way resembles all the process-ridden forms of writing belonging to Nietzsche: the fragment, *die*

---

24 *Kritische Studienausgabe* 13: 246.

Stücke, the aphorism, the letter. The "grand style" may come to mind when reading the hymnal sequences of *Zarathustra*, but they are an exception in Nietzsche's œuvre. In considering Nietzsche's writing practice, I feel instead tempted to describe it as *small style*. This is, of course, a term that Nietzsche does not use himself, considering all the prestige he invests in the "grand style". Nietzsche's "small style" is *improvisatory*, to use another term that is not used by Nietzsche; but a term that seems to designate his procedure in, for instance, the third *Abhandlung* in *Genealogy*, mentioned earlier: he "improvises" twenty-eight commentaries/variations on the motif of the preluding aphorism.

You may remember that Nietzsche, as a musician, was appreciated for his exuberant improvisations on the keyboard (while his written compositions are rather conventional). The description of an art of improvisation can be applied not only to the third *Abhandlung* from *Genealogy* but more or less *everything* that Nietzsche writes as a "free philosopher": *Beyond Good and Evil* as 296 improvisations on the theme *Beyond* divided into 9 *Hauptstücke*; *The Case of Wagner* as 12 improvisations in letters; *The Twilight of the Idols* as 10 themes that are entwined in improvised variations; *Anti-Christ* as 62 improvisations in one sequence on the anti-Christ theme – I am merely mentioning some of Nietzsche's later titles. The notebooks from the same period can also be read according to an improvisatory logic: each booklet consists of a sequence of variations on one theme or a couple of themes. Furthermore, Nietzsche seems to "compose" his thematic sequences in a kind of musical inspiration. For instance, the "epistemological" third "book" of *The Gay Science* consists of no less than 275 *Stücke* as variations on a theme, ending in a series of shorter *Stücke*, ending with 8 questions with aphoristic answers – maybe Nietzsche wanted to install a rhythmical development into "presto" (one of his favorite terms) followed by a "diminuendo" with a surprise ending. Micrologically-speaking, a similar organization can be followed in each piece: the argument undulates and sometimes includes its own opposition. The improvisatory effect is duly planned and we know that Nietzsche repeatedly polished his *Stücke*. As we have already seen, he *enumerates* his "improvisations" meaning that he feeds his "free" improvisations into some kind of system. Via its aphorisms and arrows and sentences and *Stücke* he varies while repeating. He controls his variations by enumeration, perhaps also with a "musical" composition. *Systematic improvisation* seems like an adequate description of the aesthetic profile of Nietzsche's "small style", his processual writing.

"Systematic improvisation" is of course an awkward term in roughly the same way as Heidegger's *Stücke* and Blanchot's fragments are: both have drawbacks when applied to describing Nietzsche's text. "Systematic improvisation" is a contradictory expression in similar manner as "aphoristic system" is (Karl Löwith's suggestion describing Nietzsche's way of writing[25]): the two terms diverge and exclude a homogeneous totality of the kind that Nietzsche seemed to have fancied with his "grand style". You may perhaps say that Nietzsche's improvisations hide a system and his system hides improvisations according to his *labyrinthic* logic. Meaning that the "small style" hides the "grand" just as the "grand style" hides the small. The relation appears to be a reflex action of the part and the whole in a hermeneutical circle; or the relation between aphorism and *Abhandlung* in *Genealogy*; or as a version of Nietzsche's most basic and far-reaching couple: Dionysos and Apollo.

Nietzsche's fantasy about the "grand style" is, as already mentioned, heading for a Utopian reality: with the "grand style" the words want to *become* real or they want to approach a reality that is not yet there. Nietzsche is expressing a *performative* ambition and it is in this performativity that I think we can locate the relation between the "grand style" and his stylistic practice: his "small style" with its process, repetitions, short forms and "systematic improvisation". Improvisation is, of course, a performative art working towards a realization of – and in – the moment. The "grand style" heads for eternity. Nietzsche's ambition transgresses the improvisation and aims at no less than inscribing the moment in eternity, making it permanent.

The sentence or sententious phrase (*Sentenz*) catches the elaborate temporality characterizing Nietzsche's style(s). We have noticed that already in *Human, All Too Human* Nietzsche praises the term and that as late as in *The Twilight of the Gods* he uses it as a heading for his writing. We have also seen that he uses *Sentenzen-Buch* as a sub-title for several of his imaginary book-titles. The *Sentenz* is of course short and compact, irrefutable and definite, and it establishes new meaning. Such is the stylistic and rhetorical version

---

25 *Nietzches Philosophie der ewigen Wiederkehr des Gleichen*. Hamburg: Felix Meiner 1978, p. 15.

of a term that could also be used grammatically: the sentence as a complete clause. It can be used in a juridical fashion: as the sentence that becomes effective when it is pronounced. With his *Sentenzen*, Nietzsche disseminates semantics into gestures and makes his words physical (I am using an observation of Peter Sloterdijk here[26]). The *Sentenz is* and *becomes* at the same time. It unites the momentary with the permanent, the moment of improvisation with eternity. I would think that it is the magic of the performative that makes the *Sentenz* attractive for Nietzsche when he wants to promote his "small style" into the powerful expressions of the "grand style". The *Sentenz* unites the improvisation of the "small style" with the irrefutable language of the "grand style."

While this union is attractive, it is also fatal. When the repetitions and improvisations of the "small style" are presented as the decrees of "grand style", the thinking process comes to an end: Nietzsche's prose is making a full stop, as in the "verdicts" solemnly pronounced at the end of *Anti-Christ.* The power of his argument is to be found in its process, its improvisatory and hypothetical character. Nietzsche's prose answers to a basic component in the idea of prose: not wanting to stop. His sentences are "arrows" directed to the future and they fall to the ground when they lose direction.

My concluding answer to the preluding question - Is Nietzsche writing philosophy or literature or both? – is, unavoidably, both. Nietzsche is writing both at the same time. Borrowing a term from Peter Sloterdijk[27] I would say that Nietzsche writes a *centauric* text that never conforms to the hopeless oppositions of modern literature: the oppositions between concept and form, between thought and aesthetics, between fact and fiction. The conclusion is hardly surprising and it must be added that the one side or aspect hides the other, and vice versa. It is a ceaseless hide-and-seek, not even ending when Nietzsche himself tries to put an end to it. A centaur caught in a labyrinth …

---

26 *Der Denker auf der Bühne. Nietzsches Materialismus.* Frankfurt: Suhrkamp 1986, p. 132.
27 Sloterdijk 1986, ch. 1.

Perhaps ... or?

Nietzsche's reflections on the labyrinth begin already in *Birth of the Tragedy*, where he declares that "the origin of the Greek tragedy" is lost in a "labyrinth."[28] The metaphor keeps coming up when Nietzsche approaches the fragmented origin that he associates with Dionysus and the Greek tragedies – as well as the predicament of modern man. The question is, what consequences this labyrinthic fascination has had for his thought and his writing. This question has been avoided by his commentators, including those with an interest in his style of writing. Wolfgang Groddeck, who has devoted meticulous readings to Nietzsche's dithyrambs, seems almost resigned when coming to the "labyrinth" that is the last word of "dithyramb" *The Lament of Ariadne*: the "real" meaning is "probably that every interpretation gets lost in it."[29] Eckhard Heftrich gives the most offensive commentary that I have been able to find: he describes Nietzsche's philosophy as based on a "labyrinthic experience" and declares without further argument that a passage in *Beyond Good and Evil* – nr. 230 discussing the will to appearance and disguise – is the "labyrinthic text par excellence."[30]

My own contribution will take the form of two small words that Nietzsche seems to fancy: *perhaps* (*vielleicht*) and *or* (*oder*). The last should be followed by a question-mark in order to function in the correct labyrinthic manner: making the reader take a break in his wandering through the text, think about possible directions, perhaps take a few steps back, develop the fertile confusion of reflection. I do not mean to say that these two words give the final labyrinthic version of Nietzsche's performative prose. I certainly do not want to exclude the possibility of finding labyrinthic constructions of separate aphorisms and *Stücke* and sequences. *Perhaps ... or?* may open the way for such consideration.

Both words are prominently exposed in *Daybreak*. The book actually ends with an *Or?* The word concludes the very last aphorism with the title "*We aeronauts of the spirit!*" Here, Nietzsche calls forth

---

28 *Kritische Studienausgabe*, vol. 1, p. 52.
29 Friedrich Nietzsche, '*Dionysos-Dithyramben*'. Berlin: de Gruyter 1991, II, p. 209.
30 *Nietzsches Philosophie. Identität von Welt und Nichts*. Frankfurt: Klostermann 1962, p. 205.

a spiritual brotherhood that he compares to migratory birds heading west. And he concludes:

> Whither does this mighty longing draw us, this longing that is worth more to us than any pleasure? Why just in this direction, thither where all the suns of humanity have hitherto *gone down*? Will it perhaps be said of us one day that we too, *steering westward, hoped to reach an India* – but that it was our fate to be wrecked against infinity? Or, my brothers. Or?
> – (*Daybreak*, p. 229)

It is a mighty comparison: brothers-birds-airships make up an impression of a great spiritual adventure ending up in Nothingness or in Eternity. Finally this *Or?* I would think that the question mark is essential. If we scrutinize the whole piece, we find that the headline and the following six sentences are all concluded with exclamation marks. Then comes a dash followed by six shorter sentences, all concluded by question marks. Nietzsche *gesticulates* and *conducts* with his language. The quotation shows the last questions diminishing in volume in a way that contributes to a tone of appeal. Six inciting exclamations followed by six appealing questions, reducing the speed. If the reader was carried away by the exclamations, he will start hesitating and questioning. (As Fernando Pessoa put it: "Life is the hesitation between an exclamation mark and a question mark."[31])

Nietzsche is fond of punctuation marks, specially the exclamation mark: it emphasizes his ambition to write irrefutable *Sentenzen* and suggests something of the inevitable finality of the *grand style*. But he uses the question mark just as often, appealing for agreement or questioning, asking for dialogue. With the question mark the quick step of the exclamations changes into the breaks and repetitions of the *small style*. *Or* is a word that hovers between exhortation and question when it stands alone, as it is in the aphorism concluding *Daybreak*. *Perhaps* (*Vielleicht*) is used a couple of times by Nietzsche with similar effect. In *Daybreak*, the words *Purposes? Will?* heads a paragraph discussing the relationship between chance and necessity, including the possibility that the "dice-box of chance" is shaken by "necessity." *Perhaps* our act of will is nothing but a throw of the dice:

> Perhaps! – To get out of this *perhaps* one would have to have been already a guest in the underworld and beyond all surfaces, sat at Persephone's table and played dice with the goddess herself. (*Daybreak*, p. 131)

---

31 *Livro do desassossego* nr 455.

Nietzsche is himself elaborating his *perhaps* with italics and exclamation mark in this mythological phantasy. He wants to emphasize the paradoxical configuration of chance and necessity: with the italicized *perhaps* we are invited to conjoin opposites and think the unthinkable in a virtual labyrinth.

Five years later, when writing *Beyond Good and Evil*, Nietzsche apparently remembers his suggestive *perhaps*. He embroiders the word in an early passage dealing (as always) with *opposites*. He wants us to suspect that opposites like good/evil and true/false are opposites only when seen with the worm's-eye view of the metaphysician. From a higher perspective, opposites hang together:

> It might even be possible that *what* constitutes the value of those good and honored things resides precisely in their being artfully related, knotted and crocheted to these wicked, apparently antithetical things, perhaps even in their being essentially identical with them. Perhaps! – But who is willing to concern himself with such dangerous perhapses! For that we have to await the arrival of a new species of philosopher, one which possesses tastes and inclinations opposite to and different from those of its predecessors – philosophers of the dangerous Perhaps in every sense. – And to speak in all seriousness: I see such new philosophers arising. (*Beyond Good and Evil*, p. 34)

Again, the *perhaps* implies a paradoxical joining of opposites, this time with the edge towards metaphysical epistemology and with a striking futuristic dimension. These new philosophers "of the terrible Perhaps" that Nietzsche invites us to wait for – at the same time as he can see them "emerging" – are closely related to the spiritual "airship-travelers", called "my brothers" when Nietzsche concludes *Daybreak* with an *Or?* The philosophers of the future are a version of that utopian brotherhood that recurs in Nietzsche's thinking. With their capacity for thinking the unthinkable, these brothers of the future belong to the "community of those without community" – I am borrowing from a commentary of this passage by Jacques Derrida, here (and a phrase coined by Georges Bataille).[32]

Perhaps is associated here with a paradoxical epistemological critique *and* with a Utopian community. Interestingly, it is also associated with femininity, as can be seen when consulting the different versions of this passage that the critical edition has collected in a commentary.[33]

---

32 *Politiques de l'amitié*. Paris: Galilée, 1994, p. 56.
33 *Kritische Studienausgabe* 14: 347f.

In an earlier version of the quoted passage, Nietzsche related his "terrible Perhaps-es" to the suspicion that "Truth" could be understood as a seductive woman who has cast off her veils. "Confronted with such a woman one cannot be prudent enough!" Nietzsche's preface to *Beyond Good and Evil* starts with the famous words: "supposing truth be a woman – what?" (p. 31) It is this delicate hypothesis that he develops a couple of pages further on with his "terrible Perhaps". He develops but he also hides; perhaps his *perhaps* invites us to a labyrinth of knowledge that covers up the secrets of sex and gender.

With his hesitating words *perhaps ... or?* Nietzsche invites his reader to a virtual labyrinth that allows no easy choices. Chance and necessity, good and evil, true and false appear as literally entangled with each other. Maybe man and woman consist of similar illusory opposites and difficult choices. Young Nietzsche, in *Birth of the Tragedy*, arrives at the conclusion that the "origin of Greek tragedy" is lost in a "labyrinth." The older Nietzsche, the critic and the moralist, still finds the origin to be labyrinthic and he invents a prose and a style that should invite his reader to share the same predicament. The last we know of Nietzsche, from the time of his breakdown in January 1889, is that he has lost himself in his own labyrinth and *become* labyrinthic.

II Prose and Modernity

Benjamin: Prose and Porosity[34]

The ontological impulse and the work of art

Europe in the 1930s was not solely the time of popular fronts and fascism, but also the period for the full emergence of modernism in the arts. This shaped a vital problem for aesthetical ontology: now was the time to settle what a work of art essentially is, what art could do, aesthetically, socially and politically. Walter Benjamin made the relationship between political and aesthetical modernism explicit in several essays, especially his programmatic and famous treatise, *The Work of Art in the Age of Mechanical Reproduction* from 1936. The essay had a belated break-through in the 1960s and it seems no less relevant today than it was then. The continuity in the discussion from the 1930s and the 1960s up until today seems to illustrate some problems that are inherent in modernism, particularly in relation to politics. The relation between aesthetics and politics is pertinent also in those different and still stimulating proposals for an aesthetical and literary ontology, which were suggested around the same time. In this context, I am thinking of John Dewey, in the USA, with *Art as Experience* (1934), pleading for the social importance for art (especially modern European visual art) when it comes to developing what he calls a full *experience* in its optimal social *environment*. I am also thinking of Martin Heidegger in Germany, who put down the first version of *The Origin of the Work of Art* in 1935, concluding that it is the work of art, above all poetical work, that constitutes truth and reality and thereby creates human history (Heidegger's Nazi commitment added a political dimension to his ontological speculation).

---

34 I am re-using text from my "The Work of Art in the Age of Ontological Speculation: Walter Benjamin Revisited." In *Walter Benjamin and Art*, ed. Andrew Benjamin, London: Continuum 2005.

Worthy of inclusion here also is Jean-Paul Sartre of France, who ends *The Psychology of Imagination* [*L'Imaginaire*, 1938] by asserting (in contrast to Heidegger) that the work of art has no direct relation to reality, rather it becomes art by *negating* reality. (Ten years later, in *What is Literature?*, he limits this negativity to "poetry" and claims political intervention to be the task of "prose").

The texts mentioned are certainly very different. Still, they share an antimetaphysical tenor and an ontological impulse. Likewise, they all express a mostly implicit belief in the political and social mission of art: art could be instrumental for democracy (Dewey) and should come to have an anti-fascistic use (Benjamin); it can create history (Heidegger) or become a refuge from historical reality and thereby a potential pocket of resistance (Sartre). Another example from the same period (that I shall not revisit here) is Roman Jacobson's "What is poetry?" (1933), in which he develops the mission of the Russian formalists – equally political and aesthetical – into an attempt to determine the poetical dimension of language.

These ontological efforts could also be understood as a series of attempts to conceptualize aesthetic *modernism*, which had become an epochal phenomenon in need of philosophy. Alternatively is it perhaps only today that we can see modernism historically and discover the modernist inspiration behind the ontological efforts (as well as a modernist demand for ontology)? Such an inspiration is, of course, obvious in the case of Dewey and Benjamin since they are relating actively to modernism, but I would believe that modernism is in the background also for philosophers like Heidegger and Sartre. Heidegger's prime examples are the 19th century poet Hölderlin and the 19th century artist van Gogh: both artists had vital importance for 20th century expressionism. Indeed Sartre personally, while working on *L'Imaginaire*, contributed to modernism by writing the novel *The Nausea* [*La nausée*], using the novel to insist on contingency and loss of meaning as the most important components of modern experience. And contingency was exactly what was considered as constitutive for the reality described by modernism – the reality handled by modernist prose.

What is art? Above all, what is a work of art: a whole, complete, final and definite work of art? Heidegger and Benjamin, in particular, take an interest in this question and Heidegger relates the work of art to truth: "The work's becoming a work is a way in which truth becomes and happens"; Art is "the setting-into-work of truth."[35] For Benjamin, it seems to be the other way around: the work of art is the historical category that is deconstructed by new technology and modern media. If Heidegger's work of art suggests a history that is not yet realized so to speak, while Benjamin's work of art already belongs to the past, then they still have a kind of ideality in common. Heidegger's work of art has a taste of the future and I would think that the philosopher invests, in the work of art, some of these expectations for a decisive intervention in time that he cultivated ten years earlier, in *Being and Time*. These are expectations that perhaps inspired his failed attempt as a university dean to become the *Führer* of university politics. Benjamin's work of art, on the other hand, is full of the nostalgia that he had a habit of investing in time past, staging his historical scenery almost as dramatic as Heidegger's: both were inclined to view history as a series of fatal reversals, as revolutions. In the case of Benjamin, this apocalyptical imagination goes hand in hand with the famous Messianism; while Heidegger's post War views on history seem to level off at fatalistic resignation.

I want to approach the complex scene sketched above by a closer look on Benjamin's *The Work of Art in the Age of Mechanical Reproduction*: what a work of art is, according to Benjamin, and why it is already at this time – 1936 – deteriorating.

Benjamin's Work of Art

In the first of the 15 sections of Benjamin's treatise, he states that the work of art could always be reproduced but that technical-mechanical reproduction – which he exemplifies via lithography, graphics, photography, film, gramophone –is now so radically thorough, that technology itself has "captured a place of its own among the artistic processes [*Verfahrungsweisen*]"[36]. Reproduction is therefore no longer secondary to an original, the unique originality of the work of art has simply ceased to exist.

---

35 Transl. Albert Hofstadter, in *Basic Writings*, NY: Harper & Row 1977, p. 180, 186.
36 I am quoting from Harry Zohn's translation in *Illuminations* (New York 1969), at times adjusted according to the German original in *GS* I:2 (Suhrkamp 1991). References will be given to the quoted section.

Benjamin draws his examples from the aesthetics of visuality and also from the sound. What about literature? It would seem that the first section of his thesis— art has been infiltrated by a technology that became the real productive force around 1900 – is contradicted by literature, since literature has long been produced and reproduced in printing. In another famous essay written around the same time, *The Story-Teller* [*Der Erzähler*], Benjamin thereby proclaims the art of printing to be the historical caesura that once and for all separates real and traditional narration from modern forms, that is, novels and journalism. Furthermore, in the first section that I just quoted from the treatise on the work of art, he states that the "enormous changes which printing, the mechanical reproduction of writing, has brought about in literature are well-known." Nevertheless, he maintains that the technology of reproduction does not fatally influence the literary work of art before 1900. Benjamin does not attempt to explain this lag until section 10, where he touches upon the situation for the contemporary literary culture (*Schrifttum*) and makes a small comparison between the production of film and literature.

Benjamin now states that the technology has further infiltrated the art of film than in other arts – he continues his argument in section 11, where we learn that the cameraman "penetrates deeply"into the "web" of given reality [*dringt tief ins Gewebe der Gegebenheit ein*]; film therefore breaks the control and the distance, that was the presupposition of the traditional work of art. Earlier, in a note to section 4, Benjamin stated that technological reproduction is an "external condition" to literature and painting while it is "inherent [*unmittelbar begründet*] in the technique of film production"; the film has therefore eliminated the distinction between original and copy, and, as a consequence, leveled the relation between production and consumption. In section 10, we are now told that literature, and indeed the entire literary culture, is giving way to new technology: the literary work of art is dissolved in a rapprochement between writer and reader. His evidence: around 1900, the reader of journals is activated into becoming the writer of "letters to the editor" and today, in the Soviet Union, Benjamin claims to know that "work itself is given a voice", making the literary expression an integrated part of working life and working capacity.

Benjamin seems naively optimistic on the behalf of journalistic technology. This should not, however, prevent us from reflecting on the possible meanings of his statement: that the distance between writer and reader has diminished or perhaps even disappeared, thereby eliminating an important presupposition for regarding the literary work as a work of art in the classical sense. At first sight, his view seems manifestly wrong: the conventional view of modernism as it was established in the 1930s, is that it emphasized the difference between *avantgarde* and popular culture and therefore also between the writer and reader. Perhaps Benjamin's diagnosis should not be understood as a description of contemporary reality but in terms of its utopian dimension, as an anticipation of something that could become possible? The technological development of writing could possibly confirm his expectations, since it now makes an electronic interaction between writer and reader quite possible. Moreover, conceivably such an interaction was anticipated by some branches of modernism? I am thinking, for example, of strategies developed by Brecht and the surrealist movement, both much favored by Benjamin.

I shall return to the question of whether or not Benjamin, in spite of his impossible examples, perhaps put his finger on some work-dissolving tendencies in literary modernism. Film, however, is his prime example and in section 9 he concludes that film has succeeded in nothing less than making art desert its classical characteristic: the "beautiful semblance" [*schönen Schein*]. He is alluding to the very *Schein* that Hegel claimed to be the sensory (re)presentation of the idea and that Nietzsche embraced as the only accessible reality. Again, literature is a problematic partner in Benjamin's discussion. What does *Schein* mean when it comes to literature? To translate it into sonority or rhythm, for example, would be too narrow: these are relatively limited ingredients when it comes to constituting the phenomenon we call "literature". Perhaps literature could be identified instead as "fiction"? Perhaps "fiction" could be called the most important contribution to the *Schein* that makes up "literature" and gives literature a relative autonomy?

In that case, one must conclude that Benjamin's observation – that art has finally left the *schönen Schein* behind – is in conflict with the literary realities of the 1930s. The modernist literature of the period confirmed the autonomy of the literary work of art, drawing a distinct line between fictional literature and, for instance, biography and other forms of prose referring to identifiable reality. Furthermore, fiction won prestige and gained an unrivalled position in the literary field, not unlike its position in the glory days of the

Victorian novel. Yet, perhaps Benjamin's statement about the *schönen Schein* and (indirectly) the decay of fiction, is not a description of his literary reality? Maybe Benjamin is once more aiming at a utopian ideal, anticipating a situation that should be easier to identify today? It would, of course, be just as silly today as it was in the 1930s to hold that the arts have definitely left the realm of *schönen Schein*, or that literature could or should no longer be related to fiction. On the other hand, the boundaries of fiction are no longer imperative and fiction seems less important than it was within literature – at the same time as fictional devices are regularly used in visual media, including documentary films and news reports. At first sight, this would indicate that Benjamin's diagnosis has been turned on its head: fiction and *Schein* have not lost ground at all; instead fiction has captured new ground. Although it is possible that a second viewing will adjust this perspective and reveal that fiction no longer constitutes literature and that *Schein*, just as Benjamin predicted, no longer coincides with art. We find fiction and *Schein* everywhere, meaning that they no longer delineate the boundary around art and literature. Meaning that Benjamin's treatise has not lost its actual relevance, but could be read as an invitation for a new mapping of the field of aesthetics.

Benjamin's favored term for discussing the *Schein* of art is the famous *aura*, appearing mainly in sections 2–5. Following on from that, the film is profiled as the prominent example of a non-auratic form of art. In section 4, Benjamin states that the aura of the work of art makes it into an object of ritual cult and that this is a condition for its status as an autonomous work: "the unique value of the 'authentic' work of art has its basis in ritual". He continues, in section 5, by stating that the art objects of primordial times (*Urzeit*) had magical functions due to the "absolute emphasis on its cult value". This magic was only gradually acknowledged as "work of art" and has "today" been replaced by "exhibition value" thereby giving the work of art "entirely new functions". The aesthetical function, depending on the *Schein* of art, will lose its magic sooner or later and will instead appear as "incidental" [*beiläufig*].

Those phrases that I have picked out from section 5 are part of a dramatic history: from the ritual art of "primordial times" through the period of the works of art, still based on cult, up to the art of today and pointing to the art of a future, that will give art completely new and unpredictable functions. (Benjamin suspects that the art of the future will be based on participation rather than cult.) In order to emphasize that the artistic Utopia has political dimensions, Benjamin adds a note, in which he refers to Brecht as producing "analogous reflections". Benjamin quotes Brecht: "If the concept of 'work of art' can no longer be applied to the thing that emerges once the work of art is transformed into a commodity, we have to eliminate this concept with cautious care but without fear".

If we try to imagine literature in this drama, it would appear, again at first sight, that Benjamin's story is completely misleading. It is contrary to historical common sense that autonomous literature would depend on ritual: it is by *liberating* itself from ritual that literature becomes the phenomenon that we can identify as literature – generally thought to occur from the late Renaissance onwards. Moreover, literature barely gained "autonomy" until Romanticism, if then even. Furthermore, the tendency to autonomy of the literary work of art seems to be strengthened with Modernism: in Benjamin's time, works are created as never before, Proust's *A la recherche*, Joyce's *Ulysses* and Eliot's *Waste Land*, for instance, could hardly be disconnected from the idea of an autonomous work of art. (It is different with a few of the Benjaminian favorites like Kafka and Brecht: they operate in the boundaries of the literary work of art.)

Modernist attacks on the work of art only came in the late sixties – the same sixties that discovered Benjamin and gave Brecht a renaissance – with, for instance, Umberto Eco's *opera aperta* and Roland Barthes' pamphlet "From Work to Text". Benjamin's idea of the work as obsolete was contradicted again, however: in the field of aesthetics, it was the visual arts of the 1960s that attacked the Work – I am thinking of conceptual art, "fluxus" and the simulacra of pop-art. The literary *avantgarde*, in their various ways, tried to join the attack, while ambitious film (in contrast to "movies") was instead regarded as high-class art and the maker of films celebrated as "auteur". Movie-makers and TV producers went back to Victorian novels (and thus "real works") in order to find models for contemporary soaps ... everything in order to contradict Benjamin's prognosis! Even today, it would seem premature to declare the work of art dead and there are considerable efforts to save the Work within aesthetical theory.[37] Perhaps Benjamin's diagnosis has a kind of actuality in the sense that

---

37 Karlheinz Stierle, *Ästhetische Rationalität. Kunstwerk und Werkbegriff*, München 1997.

the Work today seems even more precarious than it could have been in the 1930s. It would be an exaggeration to credit technology with the full responsibility for a historical development that is equally attributable to institutional and ideological changes. Nevertheless, it is difficult to avoid the impression that the idea of the work of art is not self-evident or functional when it comes to pictorial art. Furthermore, when fiction spills over the traditional limits of literature, the conditions of the literary work of art will be changed

When Heidegger explored the origin and essence of the work of art and proclaimed its potential as the creator of history – at the same time as Benjamin cancelled its future – he had the literary work in mind. He is using van Gogh's famously rendered shoes in order to establish his argument, but nevertheless ends up stating that the truth of being takes place by being "*gedichtet*", that *all* art is essentially *Dichtung*. It might seem as though Heidegger's work of art is to be found on another planet than Benjamin's, but I would nevertheless like to stress that they do have something in common. The difficulty in situating literature in Benjamin's technological imagination – as well as Heidegger's essential literature – has to do with the fact that the literary work of art *does not exist*. Alternatively, it exists, but only when it takes place. And who knows when it takes place? In strange ways it would seem that both thinkers point to the literary work as a *possibility* rather than an empirical reality.

The 1960s was the time for the "open" work of art – art coming out of the work – as well as for the rediscovery of Benjamin. The same applies for the thinker whom, more so than anyone else, combined Benjamin's modernist impulse with Heidegger's ontological: I am thinking of Maurice Blanchot and of the texts in the last part of *The Infinite Conversation* (1969) in particular. There, we read about the "absence of the book", the subversion of the work and it not being put into work, its *desœuvrement*. This *desœuvrement* would be the movement in the work that opens, surpasses and deconstructs the work. Like Benjamin, Blanchot regards the work of art as already dissolved due to being completed and, like Heidegger, he sees the work of art as not yet realized. In keeping with both his predecessors, he inscribes his *desœuvrement* in a dramatic historical setting. However in contrast to both Benjamin and Heidegger, Blanchot understands the realizing dissolution of the work of art as a consequence of its fundamental negativity. The ontological speculation of the 1930s culminates, with Blanchot, in a negative theology on behalf of the work of art.

Modernism and negativity

All modern efforts to determine the essence and ontology of literary work rest on a version of negativity: literature is *not* like all other linguistic communication; literature communicates *indirectly* rather than directly, literature *negates* reality on order to constitute a reality of its own, literature *kills* the real flower or the physical woman that is named in a literary manner (I am alluding to a famous figure of thought, found by Blanchot in Mallarmé and used to initiate his first large-scale discussion on the essence of literature: "Literature and the right to death", 1948). The negative characteristics of modern poetry are flourishing in the first chapter of Hugo Friedrich's *Die Struktur der modernen Lyrik* from 1956, where modern poetry is, for instance, "abnormal", "confusing", "dissolving", "incoherent", "fragmentary", "astigmatic", "alienating".

The closing of literary expression into literary *work* also follows this *via negativa*: the literary expression becomes the literary work by breaking its relations to history, society and originator. It is by negation or discontinuity that the literary work becomes an autonomous republic with a history of its own. This republic is the imaginary realm of pure literature or of *fiction*, living by virtue of its negativity. Fiction is simply the literary way to disconnect from "reality" in order to constitute a literary reality on its own.

No doubt all these versions of negativity express a strong tradition in art, literature and criticism. *So* strong that it perhaps tempts us to forget the "heteronomy" that infiltrates the "autonomy" of modern art (according to the terminology favored by Adorno), or to disregard *fragmented* or even *positive* relations; that is, a possible *continuity* between history, society and artistic expression. However, negativity has certainly dominated the poetics of modernism, as was settled in the 1950s: not only by Hugo Friedrich, but also in musical theory by Adorno, in the philosophy of literature by Blanchot, and in art criticism by Clement Greenberg. Sartre gave an important foreboding of the aesthetics of negativity in the final chapter of *L'imaginaire* (1938), while Benjamin, in his *Work of Art in the Age of Mechanical Reproduction*, appears to use both negative and positive determinations.

In the fourth section of his treatise, Benjamin speculates on the dependence of ritual for the "aura" of the authentic work of art and he includes "the 19th century idea of *l'art pour l'art*" in his argument. He explains this "doctrine" [*Lehre*] as an attempt to activate an aesthetic cult as a reaction against "the advent of the first truly revolutionary means of reproduction, photography" (the art of printing has again disappeared from Benjamin's aesthetical horizon). *L'art pour l'art* is a "theology of art", according to Benjamin, and it has developed into a "negative theology in the form of the idea of 'pure' art, which not only denied any social function of art but also every relation to concrete subject-matter". Within parentheses, Benjamin names Mallarmé as the first to have attained this position.

Meaning that the first was to be the last: because it is in the era of Mallarmé that Benjamin finds the technological changes that finally disconnect the literary work from its "aura" and therefore dissolve the work as work. The "negative theology" of Mallarmé was, in other words, not only a realization of "pure" art, but also a contribution to its dissolution. I have already punctuated this history with some question marks by trying to understand it in its utopian dimension. Of course, Mallarmé was not a last outpost in the history of the literary work of art; rather he was a pioneer for all those negative determinations that have characterized the aesthetics of modernism. Mallarmé is the starting-point for Hugo Friedrich's still unsurpassed history of modern poetry, likewise for Blanchot's attempt to conceive the work as realized in its *desœuvrement*.

When Sartre concludes *L'imaginaire* with a speculation on the ontology of the work of art, he does not mention Mallarmé. Although what Benjamin called a "negative theology" (employing a term that became current in the 1920s) would nevertheless be an apt characterization of Sartre's determination of our imaginative capacity as, exactly, negative. Sartre regards reality as a contingent flow of sensations and perceptions. "Imagination" is the act whereby the subject handles the contingency of reality and tries to grasp the reality of things as figures, as finished shapes, as closed *works*. "Thus the imaginative act is at once *constitutive, isolating* and *annihilating*."[38] By imagination, the subject "constitutes" a new reality out of the ruins of real reality; for the new one is actually no reality at all, only

---

38 I am using Mary Warnock's translation in *The Psychology of Imagination* (1972). All quotes from the first part of chapter 5:"Conclusion".

a negation of the real one, a Nothing. In the act of imagination "I grasp *nothing*, that is, I posit *nothingness*". Negation is the very condition for the "unreality" or nothingness created by imagination; the same also applies for the work of art, since art is simply the aesthetically organized version of imagination.

Sartre's strong emphasis on negation and nothingness (developed from of his reading of Hegel's *Phenomenology of Spirit*) seems like an overture to all those negative determinations that are characteristic of the aesthetics of modern art, at least in its theoretical versions. In practice – today – the negativity of modernism would not appear quite as compelling; some regard modernism as belonging to the past, while others have initiated negotiations with the *positive* components of modernist tradition. Perhaps Benjamin's more or less utopian speculation on the dissolution of the work of art could be understood as an early version of such attempts?

As we recall, Benjamin mentions "letters to the editor" and "work reports" from the Soviet Union as not particularly convincing examples in his argument (in section 10 of the treatise) for the disappearing "basic character" of the distance between writer and reader – a presupposition for the negatively determined work of art. If we manage to excuse his hopeless examples as period-bound, we may be able to regard them as Benjamin's suggestions to *positive* openings of the "negative theology", that he related to Mallarmé and that came to characterize the aesthetics of modernism. The letter and the testimonial report suggest the position of the *witness* and indicate some kind of interaction between writer and reader.

I would like to think that Benjamin is exercising a pragmatic impulse.

Prose and porosity

Benjamin is inclined to apocalyptic speculation; no doubt, this contributed to his attraction, when he was being read from the 1960s onwards by the new "left", where we were looking for categorical answers to "everything". The "pure language", the "absolute" and the catastrophically timely "moment" were fascinating ideas. Likewise, the thought that art could be changed, or had already changed perhaps, in a quite decisive manner, for itself and for the world. This weakness for grandiose gestures is still very much alive among those theorists of media – of which Friedrich Kittler is a prominent example – that, today, are developing Benjamin's notions from his treatise on the work of art: technological changes of media as instrumental for epochal changes of history. For my own part, I have, on several revisits, grown more interested in Benjamin's capacity for attentive reading, his stylistic provocations, his interest in possibilities, his nostalgic resignation confronting the passing of time, his *prose*. Perhaps it is my own (or current) pragmatism that alerts me to his interest in the functions and contexts of art and aesthetic experience. Nowadays, I like to fancy Benjamin in Paris in the 1930s as not being very far from Fernando Pessoa's melancholy observer in Lisbon, according to *The Book of Disquiet* written about the same time: both are diligent observers collecting observations, quotations and formulations, secret revolutionaries restlessly abiding the unexpected. Both *dream in prose*, to use a formula from Pessoa. Benjamin's *Work of Art in the Age of Mechanical Reproduction* appears to vacillate between the apocalyptic and the pragmatic: he expresses a strong expectation that decisive events are about to take place, or perhaps already have taken place, at the same time as he provides concrete and constructive observations on the technology, institutions and functions of art.

Among the ontologists of the 1930s, Sartre, closing the work of art in Negativity, is probably the only one to lack pragmatic elements; on the other hand, he comes back, ten years later, to language as action in *What is Literature*. Heidegger's *Origin of the Work of Art* is, of course, dominated by the ontological impulse, as are his lectures on Hölderlin from the same period. Heidegger does not condescend to reflect on the institutions of art but, when he is about to confirm the essence of art, he cannot avoid its functions – according to Heidegger, the work of art only exists when it takes place: when it functions as a creator of history and social institutions. It is the other way around with John Dewey, whom, in *Art as Experience*, derives the essence of art from its functional context. Dewey's basic thought – that only art will make it possible for man to collect his flickering sensations, his *transitory thrills*, into full *experience* – seems not so far from Benjamin's predictions about the new kinds of experiences, that are to be expected when the work of art becomes the result of intimate cooperation between producer and consumer. Benjamin may situate the art-experience in the past and he declares that "experience has fallen in value", according to a much quoted dictum from the first section of *The Story-Teller*, however, that does not stop him from expressing strong expectations for the new kinds of experience that should emerge out of new functional contexts of art. Dewey imagined the modern and fully developed work of art as a decisive component in the interaction between man and his world, the work of art being a prerequisite of an *environment* worthy of human life; Dewey is a kind of human ecologist treating art as a far too neglected part of life. It is exactly this environmental interaction between art and consumer that Benjamin explores in some of the most interesting parts of his treatise when he starts speculating on the possibilities of a new sensibility, that could provoke quite new experiences.

In section 15, Benjamin wishes to scrutinize the received idea that the large audience (the "crowd") seeks "distraction" [*Zerstreuung*]. Whoever "concentrates before a work of art is absorbed by it" [*Der vor dem Kunstwerk sich Sammelnde versenkt sich darein*]; while the "distracted" crowd absorbs the work of art (meaning that art is disseminated in the crowd). This is evident when it comes to buildings, according to Benjamin: "Architecture has always represented the prototype of a work of art with a collective and distracted reception". Nowadays, this "distracted" reception is cultivated throughout the film. Due to its "shock effect", the film subdues the cultic value that is nevertheless on the retreat in all forms of art; instead, the film cultivates sensations that are both "tactile" and "optical", combining a "discerning attitude" [*begutachtende Haltung*] with a distracted attention. "The public is an examiner, although a distracted one".

In section 14, Benjamin had argued that surrealists and dadaists had prepared the way for this new kind of reception: when facing the pictorial or literary work of the avant-garde, it is impossible to find the time for the "concentration" [*Sammlung*] that was demanded by a traditional work. Instead, such works induced in its audience a "vehement distraction" [*vehemente Ablenkung*] with the tactile qualities of a "bullet". The dadaistic shock was still wrapped up in a kind of morality, with the avant-garde wanting to cause moral disturbance; the film has liberated itself and its audience from this morality while developing the tactile shock.

I have tried to summarize this argument, where Benjamin wants to combine his favorite term from his studies of Paris and Baudelaire – the shock, the "bullet" – with the idea of distraction or dissemination as a decisive part of a new aesthetical sensibility, paving the way for a new kind of experience. When Benjamin writes about Baudelaire, it is the sensations of the *flaneur* in the street that are based on shock; and the shock is regarded as constitutive for the modern and urban experience. Now, the shock has moved forward in time: to the destruction, executed by avant-garde and film, of the traditional art reception that is named "concentration" [*Sammlung*] by Benjamin and associated to individual absorption in a kind of Kantian distance to immediate "interest". Now, the shock is characterized as a disseminated, although still intensive, distraction; the odd expression *vehemente Ablenkung* appears to be one of Benjamin's dialectical "constellations", where he tries to freeze or concentrate conflicting movements in one expression.

What could it mean? That something disseminates and distracts while being triggered by a physical and mental shock, a *vehement* shock? Why is that "symptomatic of profound changes in apperception", as Benjamin puts it in section 15: changes in perception, sensibility, experience? Furthermore, why is it that the cinema audience takes the lead in this new sensibility?

It seems difficult to answer such questions and still more difficult to locate Benjamin's versions of shock in empirical reality. In that case, the shock appears as a far too simple description of a complicated reality and as a narrow concept, that hardly covers more than some minor part of the manifold sensations, that can be experienced on the street as well as in the cinema. Instead, I suppose one should judge the shock, and especially this "distracted" shock with its *vehemente Ablenkung*, as though Benjamin is searching for alternatives to the position that the art recipient was given in the classical and Kantian tradition. Here, you were supposed to keep distance and control; Benjamin's modern consumer is instead affected by art, influenced, involved, changed, collectivized. Benjamin calls the classical position a concentrated *Sammlung*, the modern a distracted *Ablenkung*. An interaction between concentration and dissemination is actually going on in *all* reception of art and Benjamin tries to accelerate this interaction by approaching the opposites towards each other, in paradoxical constellations like *vehemente Ablenkung*; likewise with this final determination of the modern film audience as "an examiner, although a distracted one".

In expressions like these, we can study how Benjamin himself puts together, concentrates, makes a *Sammlung*. Such is his style, his *prose*, to use a term that Benjamin used in his early work on the art criticism of German Romanticism and called the "idea of poetry": "the notion of the idea of poetry as prose determines the whole art philosophy of Romanticism".[39] I suppose that Benjamin had a more sober view of "prose" some fifteen years later, but also that he had refined his own version of prose: to concentrate [*sammeln*] his distracted, contingent impressions of modern art and his experience of modern reality into paradoxical verbal constellations. Doing this was a modernist project with pragmatic implications: Benjamin tried to give his readers a "shock", one that should dissolve received notions and make room for something new. To concentrate what is contingently disseminated: that is indeed a definition of the tendency I call modern prose!

Thus Benjamin's stylistic praxis could be regarded as a pragmatic version of modernist prose; as his effort to find an alternative to the "negative theology" of the Mallarmé-tradition.

But when he calls for this *vehemente Ablenkung*, he moves beyond stylistics: in this constellation, there is a glimpse of an experience that exceeds the field of aesthetics. It is a "dionysiac" fascination for a collectivity without subjects; "dionysiac" in the Nietzschean sense, as an ecstatic surpassing of individual identity. Benjamin seems to idealize the distracted dissemination of individuality at the expense of its *Sammlung*. Such fascination keeps coming back in his work. In the essay "Naples", which Benjamin wrote ten years earlier together with Asja Lacis, the key words are *porosity* and the *porous,* meaning that the limits of the subject become flexible and conditioned by social context.[40]

Benjamin's "porosity" of 1925 prefigures the *flaneur* culture he was to localize in 19th century Paris, as well as the disseminated distraction he finds in the cinema of 1935 and associates with avant-garde expressions of art. Naples is, of course, described as a pre-modern precinct, a *Gemeinschaft* in contrast to modern *Gesellschaft.* This is not necessarily one of Benjamin's many contradictions, it can instead be understood as a constant fascination with a "dionysiac" dissolution of the subject. One can perhaps say (indeed as I started to say earlier) that in this way Benjamin strives for diminishing the distance between art and audience, preparing for the ideas of an "open" work of art, for instance, as it was understood in the 1960s. However, Benjamin's fascination could *also* be associated to the kind of social

---

39 *Der Begriff der Kunstkritik in der deutschen Romantik. GS* I:1, p. 103. My translation. There is more on Benjamin's idea of "prose" in the following chapter on Adorno.
40 *GS* IV:1, p. 305–316.

collectivity that was developed in the 1930s with fascistic pretexts. Benjamin's political aim, with the treatise on the work of art, was of course to provide an alternative to fascism; although there are still elements of his "dionysiac" fascination for a *Gemeinschaft* beyond individuality that cannot entirely be separated from the ideologies of collectivity: a fact of his own time.

Perhaps such associations could be avoided if instead we call Benjamin's recurrent fascination a pragmatic impulse. Benjamin is a pragmatist in the sense that he makes individuality as well as art experience dependant on its functional context. The "porosity" of Naples and the shock of Paris both contribute to the *vehemente Ablenkung* of the avant-garde. These versions of distraction pave the way for the distracted examiner that Benjamin believes is to be found in the cinema. A common factor in the examples is that context and function are decisive for the experience to be expected and also for the individual experience. While Benjamin may appear to exclude experience as well as individuality and the traditional work of art from the contexts that he finds attractive in Naples and Paris and modernity; he nevertheless also anticipates new and unknown forms of aesthetical work and individual experience.

When Benjamin insists on the importance of technology and context it means that he modifies his ontological impulse as well as his apocalyptic tendencies; the ontology is pragmatically modified and apocalypse fades into a glimmer of possibilities. He may contribute to the "negative theology" that is to become the modernist aesthetical ontology of the 1930s, but he also goes beyond negativity on behalf of the new and as yet unknown functions and possibilities of an aesthetical environment. His individual is already completely disseminated, since traditional experience has fallen in value. But the disseminated individuals are open to new experience and the "porosity" of their lives makes it possible for them to adapt, improvise, play and experiment with their own boundaries, prefiguring postmodern constructions. His work of art may be sentenced to the museal detention of lost aura, still aesthetical activity adapts to new forms: the image is being copied, filmed and spread in new ways. The literary work becomes letters, testimonies and documents – or perhaps the documents become literary? Benjamin's prose is never conclusive; its porosity makes it possible for us to overcome the shock and distract our thoughts with the possibilities of the future.

Adorno: Concentric Prose[41]

In this chapter, I shall give a brief presentation of Adorno's efforts to find an adequate form of expression, a style that fits his experiences of exile, the German disaster and the great tradition of critical thinking and modernist aesthetics. I shall concentrate on his essayistic and aphoristic *Minima Moralia* but also make some excursions to a few of his poetological statements. I shall also touch upon the connections to his predecessor in matters of modernist prose: Walter Benjamin. This will give me the opportunity to speculate on modernist prose and the metaphysics of prose.

Minima Moralia

Adorno published *Minima Moralia* in 1951, a book based on the German-Jewish intellectual's experiences during his American exile. The subtitle – "Reflections from damaged life" – indicates that the critical stance is close to the one in *Dialectics of Enlightenment*, written together with Max Horkheimer while they were still in the USA. However, the subtitle also tells us that we are to read "reflections" that are more intimate than the broad perspectives in the earlier book. *Minima Moralia* altogether consists of 153 "reflections", divided in three sections. The "reflections" vary in length but they are all compact and aphoristic and bear fancy titles, probably inspired by Walter Benjamin's aphoristic *Einbahnstraße [One Way Street]*.

The book is preluded by a "Dedication" (to Max Horkheimer), emphasizing the exile as the point of departure: "In each of the three parts the starting-point is the narrowest private sphere, that of the

---

41 I am reusing elements from the essay "Adorno's Prose" in *Estetikk. Sansing, erkjennelse og verk*, ed. Bente Larsen, Oslo: Unipub 2006.

intellectual in emigration."[42] The theme returns in several "reflections", for instance number 13: "Every intellectual in emigration is, without exception, mutilated, and does well to acknowledge it to himself, if he wishes to avoid being cruelly apprised of it behind the tightly-closed doors of his self-esteem." (*Minima* Moralia, p. 33) And in number 35 we learn that a German intellectual had to depart into "inner exile" long before the Nazis forced them to leave the country. Adorno is also airing what is to be a grand theme of the book: the disappearance of a worthy life under the pressure of a totalizing consumer state: "What the philosophers once knew as life has become the sphere of private existence and now of mere consumption, dragged along as an appendage of the process of material production, without autonomy or substance of its own." (*Minima Moralia*, p. 15) Not only a worthy life has disappeared, but also the individual itself – the traditionally independent and responsible combination of *homme* and *bourgeois*: "the individual has gained as much in richness, differentiation and vigour as, on the other hand, the socialization of society has enfeebled and undermined him." (*Minima Moralia*, p. 17) Adorno's frequent lamentation over loss gives the book a nostalgic character that is balanced by the furious critical stance, exemplified by details and structures from contemporary life. The alleged loss of authenticity, integrity, totality and so forth also motivates Adorno's critical style. He explains in the "Dedication" that Hegel's *Phenomenology* is the methodical model of *Minima Moralia* although he is, of course, skeptical about Hegel's "claim to totality" – the fragmentary form is the stylistic version of his skepticism.

The fragmentary style of *Minima Moralia* contributes to a constant theme in Adorno's thinking: how to find a way of writing that is adequate to the modern experience of a world that has gone to pieces and a truth that is beyond comprehension. Adorno's influential position as a propagator of modernist aesthetics in music and literature and aesthetical theory is underpinned by his development of a modernist *prose* – bolder in *Minima Moralia* than, for instance, in the unfinished *Ästhetische Theorie* or the many *Noten zur Literatur,* that tend to be more traditionally essayistic.

---

42   *Minima Moralia*, transl. E.F.N. Jephcott, NLB 1974, p. 18. Reference will be given in the text.

Close to the centre

In order to approach Adorno's poetics of prose, I shall take a look at some of his poetological statements, starting with *Minima Moralia* nr 44. There, we read the demand: "In a philosophical text all the propositions ought to be equally close to the centre [*sollte alle Sätze gleich nahe zum Mittelpunkt stehen*]." (*Minima Moralia*, p. 71) The context makes it clear that Adorno is aiming at a kind of phenomenological poetics: the thing itself should come to words in the philosophical text, without the slightest bit of mediation or any contextual support. Remarkably, he also states that Hegel came close to such a prose, although the Hegelian effect was limited by Hegel's defense of the subject as, exactly, subject. The task would therefore be to write as Hegel without the Hegelian subject..

In another aphorism, nr 51 (starting part II), he declares: "Properly worked texts are like spiders' web: tight, concentric, transparent, well-spun and firm." (*Minima Moralia*, p. 87) Texts should be "concentric". All sentences should be "equally close to the centre". This is a fascinating while also puzzling idea. What could it mean? Perhaps it means a very lapidary prose built on apodictic sentences, all directly emanating from the topic treated, the thing itself as the centre. Since Adorno excludes all subjectivity from his poetics, it could not be any sentences pronounced by a profiled subject, but rather subject-free judgments and sentences magically derived from the thing itself. It is not difficult to associate this ideal with Adorno's own prose, which could hardly be called systematic. Adorno rarely uses the many subordinate clauses made possible by the German language or even cares for constructing logically motivated sequences. Instead, his prose makes an oral impression and comes close to a swift and compact telegraphic style, although never appearing subjective or sentimental. However, whether or not he is writing as philosophical texts should be written, according to his own demand remains to be answered. After all, Adorno states, that "all propositions" *ought to be* "equally close to the centre"; and that indicates that his ideal expresses exactly that, an ideal. This ideal returns as soon as he touches poetics; which I want to demonstrate by visiting two later texts with poetological impact: *The Essay as Form* and *Parataxis*. Before returning to *Minima Moralia*, I shall compare these texts with some passages on the phenomenon of prose found in Adorno's admired predecessor: Walter Benjamin.

The Essay as Form is one of Adorno's formidable pieces from the 1950s making light work of philosophical enemies such as Heidegger. Although Heidegger is not mentioned by name, it is certainly he whom is the target when Adorno chides the hopeless efforts to get rid of the opposition between subject and object in the hope that Being itself would come to words. (Adorno may not remember that his own ideal demands that the thing itself should come to words or at least be the "centre" for all sentences.) Adorno is also critical of academics that cannot tolerate an essayistic performance and suspects them of being positivists – we are approaching the so-called *Positivismusstreit*. Essayistic thought and essayistic form is, rather, critical in itself, nothing less than "the critical form *par excellence.*"[43] What he calls the *emphatic* essay (in contrast to those despicable versions to be found in journalism as well as in Heideggerian philosophy) bears the full consequences of "critique of the system." ("The Essay as Form", p. 98) The essay is systematically critical and is critical of any system. The essay is "accentuating the fragmentary, the partial rather than the total." ("The Essay as Form", p. 98) The essay even "negates" all versions of the System; it "cancels" academic and systematic demands for completeness and continuity, *Vollständigkeit und Kontinuität*. The essay could never be a Whole, nor could it be a completed work. The essay cultivates a *Diskontinuität*, which makes it possible to express a reality that is full of conflict and lacking reconciliation.

With persuasive flair, Adorno situates the essayist as being lonely-but-strong. It seems idiosyncratic to call the essay, as Adorno calls it: an immanently "critical" form, even "the critical form *par excellence.*" That cannot easily be combined with the essayistic tradition from Montaigne (even though Adorno, as everyone else discussing the essay, claims a heritage from Montaigne). Montaigne's version of the essay, as discussed in my first chapter, could be called skeptical and perhaps asystematic but hardly "critical". *Kritik* is Adorno's own and favorite word and agenda, he seems to correlate the critical potential of the essay with its value and its value with its being exclusive and being exclusively critical. His characteristics of the essayistic text, yielding drastic wordings, can accept hardly any essays as essays.

---

43 The Essay as Form", transl. Bob Hullot-Kentor & Frederic Will, *The Adorno Reader*, Blackwell 2000, p. 106. Reference will be given in the text.

The essays in this book, for instance, would not be called essayistic and therefore not critical; I would never permit myself to negate *all* systematics, nor would I ever even attempt to cancel all academic demands in order to cultivate a discontinuous text – in fact, I doubt that even Adorno's own text comes up to his ideal. Which would demonstrate, again, that it is an *ideal* that is suggested by Adorno under the heading "essay". Therefore, it is not surprising to find the return of the demand from *Minima Moralia* – all propositions "equally close to the centre" – now adjusted into a program for the essay: the essay, we read, is sovereign in relation to facts and theory because for it (the essay), "all objects are equally near the centre" ("The Essay as Form", p.107). Adorno's ideal essay-writer has actually seen through the notion of a privileged centre and thereby the notion of the genuine and the authentic, the Whole and the systematic also. This makes the essayist in Adorno's version distinct from academics and metaphysicians, as well as from teachers of "creative writing", recorder-playing and finger-painting – to mention but a few of those uncritical, un-essayistic and vulgarly ontological activities expressly despised by Adorno.

Adorno's prose verges on essayistic prose – in his own ideal form – but also on poetical prose. This becomes clear in his discussion of Hölderlin's hymnical poetry, in the essay "Parataxis" from the 1960s.[44] When demanding "coordination" from the essay – "it co-ordinates elements, rather than subordinating them" ("The Essay as Form", p. 109) – he actually defines what he approaches as the paratactical style, typical of Hölderlin's late poetry. Parataxis means that the grammatical clauses are coordinated on the same level rather than being syntactically subordinated (and subordination comes easier than coordination in German). No doubt, Adorno points to something important in Hölderlin's "hymnical" effort and the essay is correctly counted as a modern classic among Hölderlin-commentaries. However, it is also evident that Adorno is again formulating an ideal that is very much his own. When he is talking about the paratactical "principle of form" as an *Antiprinzip* with a critical potential, although we are far from Hölderlin, we are reminded of his tribute to the essay as critical and "anti-systematic". When he (against all philological reason) declares the Hölderlinian hymn to be beyond completion, *konstitutiv unvollendbar*, he is characterizing the essay

---

44 *Noten zur Literatur III*, Frankfurt: Suhrkamp 1965, p. 156–210.

rather than the hymn: the "emphatical essay", where everything is "equally near the centre," is governed by a kind of additive principle of form, where any amount of sentences can be added without continuity or conclusion. The essay, as well as the Hölderlinian poem, is not a completed work. Furthermore, when he writes that Hölderlin sacrifices the grammatical period in a form of violence against language, *Gewalt wider die Sprache*, again, we are close to the ideal essay, that, according to Adorno, cancels out grammatical and systematical continuity – we are even closer when he states that Hölderlin thereby shakes the category of meaning, *die Kategorie des Sinnes*, that is, the very category attacked by the critical essay.

With *Parataxis*, Adorno wants to arrest Hölderlin in his development from the traditionally metrical poetry into the free rhythm of the hymns; he calls the result *prose*. The hymn "configurates" the "pure language" that "according to the holy texts should be prose." The subjunctive mood, together with the solemn wording, indicates that Adorno is once more aiming at an unattainable ideal, or an "idea" being "con-figurated" by Hölderlin's hymnical fragments. He may miss the mark as far as Hölderlin is concerned, but he is certainly saying something significant about his own prose.

Adorno's prose as Benjamin's prose

The philosophical text, that should allow all its parts to stand "equally close to the centre", and the essayistic text, where everything is "equally near the centre", are approaching a "pure language" that "should be prose" according to the Hölderlin-essay. Prose! I would think that Adorno has Walter Benjamin in mind here. Already by the 1920s, and the preceding decade even, Benjamin had made some now famous speculations on "pure language" and the "pure word". He also associates these phenomena with Hölderlin's hymnical poetry (it was published to great effect by Norbert Hellingrath from 1913). Adorno could also have picked up words such as "configuration" and "constellation" from Benjamin, who employed exactly those terms in order to signify the kind of representation that resists continuity, subordination, closure and reconciliation – Benjamin called the result "dialectical images" and "frozen dialectics": *Dialektik im Stillstand*.

In my chapter on Benjamin, I mentioned that his idea of prose was inaugurated in his early treatise on German Romanticism, *Der Begriff der Kunstkritik in der deutschen Romantik*. I shall elaborate this observation here in order to emphasize Benjamin's importance for Adorno. Benjamin declares that "the idea of poetry is prose"[45] and quotes Novalis in order to confirm that poetry is the prose of the arts: "Poetry is the prose among the arts." (*Der Begriff der Kunstkritik*, p. 102) Benjamin regards this singular statement as a decisive and still productive contribution to the romantic philosophy of art as a whole, and he praises Hölderlin for having understood and applied the idea of prose. Like Adorno, he is thinking of Hölderlin's hymnical poetry but also of his poetological letter to Böhlendorff from 1801, with its statement on the sobriety (*Nüchternheit*) of art. Benjamin seems to mean that Hölderlin with his "sobriety" points to the conditions of poetry and art as being prosaic reality, the very reality that Hegel, in his lectures on aesthetics, called "the prose of reality."[46] However, sober prose also points to the critical reflexion, that would dissolve poetry into prose by bringing it nearer the "prosaic essence" of the poetical work. (*DerBegriff der Kunstkritik*, p. 109) "Prose", in other words, is the presupposition of literary language, but also a vehicle for its purpose and consummation.

On a couple of occasions, Benjamin returns to the hopeful thought that Hölderlin comes close to that "pure language" he calls "prose" in his hymnical poetry. In his ambitious treatise on the origin of the German tragedy, he picks up Hölderlinian "sobriety" once more, and in his later speculations on the philosophy of history "prose" is again a key term. Here is a fragment written, according to Benjamin's editor, in the vicinity of his last accomplished work from 1940, *On the Concept of History* [*Über den Begriff der Geschichte*], and called "The dialectical image" ("Das dialektische Bild"). I have translated the relevant parts:

> If you want to regard history as a text, then you have to do what a later writer said about the literary text: the past has located pictures in this text, that could be compared to a plate that is sensible to light. /---/ The historical method is a philology that is based upon the book of life. 'To read what was never written', according to Hofmannsthal. The reader we are talking about is the true historian.

---

45 *Der Begriff der Kunstkritik in der deutschen Romantik. Gesammelte Schriften* I: 1, Frankfurt: Suhrkamp 1991, p. 101. Reference will be given in the text.
46 G.W.F. Hegel, *Werke* 14, Frankfurt: Suhrkamp 1990, p. 219.

> The plurality of histories reminds us of the plurality of languages. Universal history, in the modern sense, could only be a type of Esperanto. The idea of a universal history is a messianic one. /---/ Its language is integral prose, which has burst the fetters of writing and will be understood by all people (like the language of birds by Sunday children). – The idea of prose coincides with the messianic idea of universal history (the versions of literary prose as the spectrum of the universally historian /---/).[47]

In this fragment, Benjamin speculates on the "text" of History as the book of life that will never be read to its end and on the language of "universal history" as "prose". His "prose" has not only a poetological perspective, as in the early treatise, but has also become "messianic": it is only when "everything" exists in a unanimous "now" (*allseitiger und integraler Aktualität*) that one can talk about an accomplished "universal history." In the historical setting in which we live, "universal history" is a mere possibility or a dimension, that can be glimpsed in our linguistic and cultural multiplicity, or perhaps find expression in artificial ways ("Esperanto"). In a Utopian perspective, however, "universal history" can be expressed and understood by everyone in a unanimous language, a language Benjamin calls "prose". He writes *integrale Prosa;* the adjective emphasizes that prose is an integrating activity, making simultaneous and concurrent what would otherwise be fragmentary. In Benjamin's "universal history" *everything* is connected; but since it is impossible to reach this destination in real history one might as well say that our world, here and now, is ruled by contingency: *everything* is temporary and accidental and lacks definite meaning.

Adorno may have had passages like this in mind when he, in "Parataxis", associated the "pure language" of Hölderlin's hymns with the "prose" of the "holy texts". He may also have been considering theories that try to trace the origin of literary prose to medieval liturgical habits, where verse (trope) means change and break, while prose means continuity and sequence, for example by extending the final vowel in a *Halleluja*, to make it introduce the following sequence.[48] In both cases, the origin and meaning of "prose" can be described as an assembling and ordering strategy. Modern prose could perhaps be summarized as a monumental effort to assemble impressions in order to handle an existence characterized by radical fragmentation,

---

47 *Anmerkungen*, in *Gesammelte Schriften* I: 3, Frankfurt: Suhrkamp 1991, p. 1238.
48 I am borrowing the example from the chapter on the relation of poetry and prose in Henri Meschonnic, *Critique du rythme* (Paris: Verdier 1982).

dissemination, contingency and lack of foundation as well as substance and totality – an effort to establish order in the chaos of reality, construct meaning out of the meaningless.

In the chapter on Benjamin, I described Benjamin's stylistic practice as a "pragmatic version" of the modernist prose that he is approaching with his ideas on, precisely, "prose". A similar principle operates with Adorno' paratactical prose. It is no secret that Adorno stands manifestly in the tradition of modernism and that accordingly he insists on the "negative" and "critical" stance inherent in modernism. I should like to add his musical schooling to this modernist profile. The serial music, derived from Schönberg and Alban Berg, was expressly meant as "musical prose".[49] The term was coined in the vicinities of Wagner but was picked up by Arnold Schönberg preparing his development of an "atonality", where all components (all twelve elements of the scale chosen) were equally important and their interrelation was crucial. Musical prose, in Schönberg's version, was an immense effort to handle (and fight) musical contingency and transform music into a significant language. Schönberg regarded prose according to the principle articulated by Friedrich Schlegel in one of his fragments: "in true prose everything must be underlined."[50]

Much better than philosophy, essay and poetry, it was serial music that accomplished those stern demands made by Adorno: coming "close to the centre". The twelve tones chosen are equivalent, no single tone is subordinated. Serial music is paratactical so to speak and it presents itself as prose. Serial music simply does exactly what Adorno claims that philosophical language should do; or what he tries to do himself throughout all his writing and most predominantly in *Minima Moralia*.

Minima Moralia nr 29

Minima Moralia bears a subtitle that is already mentioned: "Reflections from damaged life". Nr 29 (p. 49f.) is perhaps the most "damaged" of all 153 "reflections": it consists of 17 aphoristic sentences devoid of any apparent connections or logical development. The title is "Dwarf

---

[49] For a overview of "musical prose": Carl Dahlhaus, *Musikalischer Realismus*, München: Piper 1982.
[50] "In der wahren Prosa müsse alles unterstrichen sein." *Athenäumsfragment* 395.

fruit", *Zwergobst*. The title may allude to the aphoristic presentation or, simply, to the 17 sentences being leftovers. The first five sentences have a nationalistic theme in common. The first is praising Proust – this is perhaps a hint of this constellation of aphorisms "reflecting" the whole since nr 1 in *Minima Moralia* is called "For Marcel Proust". The second compares French painting with German (to the advantage of the French). A thrust against "Anglo-Saxon countries" is followed by a surprising compliment on the sublime American landscape and a glimpse from the exile.

The following three sentences convey a vaguely psychological theme: psychoanalysis, happiness, dreams. Then, four sentences follow with historical dimensions: the last one mentions Hegel and employs a brief quote from *Phenomenology of Spirit*. Adorno tells us that the consciousness of the self that had some meaning in Hegel's day has been lost: "Today self-consciousness no longer means anything but reflection on the ego as embarrassment, as realization of impotence: knowing that one is nothing." (Perhaps Adorno had practiced his English by reading Emily Dickinson while he was in the USA: her poem nr 288 starts like this: "I'm Nobody! Who are you?")

The last, short sentences seem to be variations on the theme of self-consciousness; while the very last, and shortest, states the following: "The whole is the false." This is, of course, a reversal of Hegel's famous dictum of Truth being a characteristic of the "Whole". Adorno's reversal could be seen either as a critique of Hegel or as a historical commentary, prepared by the earlier sentence on the changes of the Hegelian idea of self-consciousness, or indeed both of these. Perhaps we should infer that a notion of the "Whole" belies the experience of a "damaged" life? Perhaps it means that contemporary truth is just as "damaged" and fragmented as contemporary life?

The fragmentary presentation distinguishes this paragraph from most of the other 152 paragraphs in *Minima Moralia*, which instead are compact monads ordered in three parts: with 50 in the first two, 53 in the last. Of course, I cannot know why Adorno used this particular number, although I am tempted to guess that he added three extra in the last section in order to prevent a harmonizing closure and perhaps also to instigate the mysterious relation, tempted by the fact that 153 is divisible by 17. Perhaps he is hinting at a serial technique in prosaic form, where all sentences are equally close to an abstract and numerical centre?

The 17 pieces of nr 29 can be read as 17 independent aphorisms but they can also be coordinated – configurated – without being subordinated into a logical or hierarchical structure. The critique of the contemporary self could perhaps be called the thematic centre here, as in all of *Minima Moralia*. The point is, of course, that the centre consists of an absence, or paradox, or broken totality: the self is no longer there. The culminating conclusion, "The whole is the false," is saying exactly that: there is no totality and every presentation claiming or presupposing or aiming at a totality, is false.

Regarded as a conclusion, it is a manifestly negative conclusion. In declaring that the Hegelian "whole" is false, Adorno also says that everything related to the "whole" – validity, substance, truth, historical meaning – is false. It means that Adorno claims validity for a conclusion while saying that such validity does not or should not exist. Aphorisms – statements – fragments in this vein are certainly not unusual in Adorno's writings. In *Minima Moralia* nr 143 we read that, "The task of art today is to bring chaos into order." (*Minima Moralia*, p. 222) The formula returns in his *Aesthetic Theory* from 1969.[51] In the same work, he declares the aesthetical and critical mission to be to comprehend the incomprehensible: "The task of aesthetics is not to comprehend artworks as hermeneutical objects; in the contemporary situation, it is their incomprehensibility that needs to be comprehended." (*Aesthetic Theory*, p. 118) Furthermore, he asks us to look for something, in art, that does not exist: "In each genuine artwork something appears that does not exist." (*Aesthetic Theory*, p. 82) All these statements are manifestly negative but they seem dialectically negative: Adorno is trying to keep a space open where observations can be made and conclusions can be drawn. He wants, in the words of Martin Seel, to open up a space of freedom: "For Adorno, art thus becomes the hallmark indicating that the world has not been comprehended if it is known only conceptually; that the world has not been appropriated if it is appropriated only technically."[52]

That is the space that I would like to delineate as Adorno's prose. In paragraph 29 of *Minima Moralia*, we read a miniature example of this prose. The 17 elements can be read as verses or tropes within a totality, that could perhaps be called a philosophical prose-poem.

---

51 *Aesthetic Theory*, transl. Robert Hullot-Kentor, London: Athlone 1997, p. 93. Reference will be given in the text.
52 Martin Seel, *Aesthetics of Appearing*, transl. John Farrell, Stanford University Press 2005, p. 15.

Or even a philosophical *haiku*: a *haiku* should configure 17 syllables within a couple of lines, culminating in a paradoxical balance. In this case we do not, of course, read 17 syllables but 17 elements, all of them just as close to the centre – a centre that does not exist, or is false, if centre signifies totality and meaning. Of course, Adorno is not writing poetry, but he is writing prose in order to state the truth as negation, in order to suggest a totality that repudiates all totality.

In another aphorism from *Minima Moralia*, nr 142, Adorno declares that "the putting together of each sentence contributes to the decision whether language as such, ambiguous since primeval times, will succumb to commercialism and the consecrated lie that is part of it, or whether it will make itself a sacred text." (*Minima Moralia*, p. 222) Again, Adorno evokes the aim of a "prose" that is also a "sacred text" (this time it is said to call for "lingusitic quixotry") which is perhaps another way of saying that it is a Utopia: this prose is a permanent reminder of a state and a centre that does not exist. Like Hölderlin's hymns, this prose "configurates" the "pure language" that cannot be anything but prose – like the serial music, this prose should be a reminder of every wordly melody but still dissociate from the world in a foreboding of the absolute and spherical music. This prose approaches an essence, a totality and a truth that is no longer there. It is certainly close to the "integral prose" that Benjamin was invoking in the fragment quoted above; to get a glimpse of it we have to read according to Benjamin's recipe: we have to read "what was never written." Perhaps Adorno is always writing a prose that invites us to read between the lines and to look for an absent truth and a fragmented whole.

The starting-point, along with the perspectives of this prose, seems to be hopeless: to assemble what cannot be assembled except in a lie; to state what only can be stated negatively, to make present what has to remain absent. One might think that such predicaments could prove devastating for the expressive capacity. But, as we all know, it works the other way round. Think of Nietzsche, who became incredibly productive at the very moment that he realized that truth and meaning were not existing entities; rather, something to be invented and produced, and invented again. Likewise with Adorno, who develops an astonishing productivity in a prose that never tires of insisting on the impossibility of its tasks. His *Minima Moralia* therefore conveys, like all his writing, an eloquent and even a comprehensive and consummate expression of the painful contradictions and paradoxes of existence. Perhaps, as Martin Seel hopes (as quoted above), he even opens a space of freedom. Perhaps his aphoristic, essayistic, paratactical and finally negative prose is a means of enduring the unendurable conclusion: *The whole is the false.*

Prose as Poetry, Poetry as Prose

In this chapter, I shall discuss two contemporary prose poems: one translated from Swedish and written by Tomas Tranströmer; and one by the Afro-American poet, Harryette Mullen. The hypothesis is, simply, that the prose poem offers an interesting version of modern prose as a literary strategy exploring the boundaries of prose as well as poetry. I will take a Nietzschean point of departure in order to give the literary analysis an epistemological and moral dimension. The prose poem is, of course, a small part of the phenomenon under investigation: prose. Nevertheless, the prose poem indicates what I call the "prosification" of modern poetry as well as modern reality.

*

In *The Gay Science*, aphorism 92, Nietzsche develops a fascinating view on the phenomenon of *prose*. "One writes good prose only *face to face with poetry*! For this is an uninterrupted, courteous war with poetry: all its attractions depend on the fact that poetry is constantly evaded and contradicted." Good prose therefore demands an active relation to what is not prose: to poetry. If you only can think in prose, you will become what Nietzsche calls a "man of prose" [*Prosenmensch*] and such men write bad prose. "*War is the father of all good things*, war is also the father of good prose."[53] Nietzsche has Heraclit in mind and his "war" translates the Greek (and Heraclitean) *polemos* – a word that can indeed mean war but also polemics, opposition, interchange, interaction.

Nietzsche's suggestion may be regarded as a cheeky comment on what had become a commonplace in his day: prose as an expression of the very conditions of modern reality. This figure of thought was summarized by Hegel. In his lectures on aesthetics from around

---

53 Transl. Josefine Nauckhoff, Cambridge University Press, 2001, p. 90.

1830, Hegel discusses the literary prose that he met in the modern novel as corresponding to "the prose of reality."[54] Hegel's observation (mentioned in the preceding chapter) was pertinent: prose, regarded as the fundamental condition of modern life and the very structure of modern reality, was actually of great importance for the development of the novel. There is a distinct line of thought from Hegel to, for instance, Flaubert, who tried to find adequate expression for prosaic reality, right up to the catchy title the philosopher Maurice Merleau-Ponty gave to one of his works from the 1950s: *La prose du monde*.

The concept of the world and its reality as prosaic prose hides an idea of poetry as an indication of a very different reality. According to Hegel, this poetry had finally lost its possibilities in the prosaic realities of bourgeois society: Hegel predicts the "end of the epoch of art". Although that does not stop the idea of a poetical alternative to reality from a more or less eternal return: as poetry, art, dream, Utopia, phantasy. Such ideas are aired once more in Nietzsche's vitalizing "war" between poetry and prose. There is also an obvious link between Nietzsche and Benjamin's "messianic" prose, as touched upon in chapter 4 (Benjamin actually quotes Nietzsche's passage on prose/poetry in one of his first speculations on prose.[55]). I believe the connection can be traced back to one of the origins of literary prose: the liturgical joining together. Nietzsche's prose does not join: it interacts. Benjamin's messianic prose finds new connections, makes a whole out of fragments and integrates what is disintegrated, transforming the necessities of preexisting connections into possibilities.

In Nietzsche's version, prose is not the Hegelian "prosaic reality" but a struggle with that reality. Prose, for Nietzsche, was a continuous activity, not a symptom or a result. Prose had little to do with either the necessities of everyday or the confinements of social structure. Instead, prose was the kind of writing that was motivated by poetry while forgoing or renouncing poetry. Prose was a way of handling and enduring a reality that poetry evades – "prose" was simply making a guest performance in Nietzsche's moral philosophy. This happened in the beginning of the 1880s and when Nietzsche speaks of "poetry" he is thinking of, for instance, Heine and Hugo. When he is talking about a "courteous war" against poetry, he may have been inspired by a relatively new phenomenon: the prose poem.

---

54 "Prosa der Wirklichkeit." *Werke* 14, FfM: Suhrkamp 1970, p. 219.
55 *Der Begriff der Kunstkritik in der deutschen Romantik. GS* I:1, p. 102.

Nietzsche read and admired Baudelaire, whose *Petits Poèmes en Prose* were published in different newspapers before they were made into a collection in 1869.

The prose poem began its literary career in the very same way that prose in general did: as a "translation" into continuous prose of what had once been poetry. With Baudelaire came a new start preparing the modern development of poetry. Nietzsche's observations can actually be read as a characteristic of the kind of prose poem – and of prosaic poetry – that would become (and still remains) an important literary strategy between the prose of fact and the prose of fiction. Clearly Nietzsche should not be read as a literary historian with prophetic insights; he wrote in order to develop a positively prosaic attitude to reality, a moral stance that he later presented as an *affirmation* of all that is. (This stance is also of importance for the Tranströmer prose poem that I shall shortly read.)

Baudelaire's prose poems (which I take to be Nietzsche's closest inspiration) differ widely from what will be exemplified below as modern prose poetry and what came to be known as poetical prose from the 1890s and onwards. Baudelaire's *Petits Poèmes en Prose* are anecdotal and can culminate in drastic, frequently sarcastic and paradoxical points. (Not unlike some of Nietzsche's prose). Baudelaire does not make poetry out of a prosaic reality, instead he shapes prose out of a romanticized or idealized or poetical version of reality. Accordingly he tends to degrade and reduce classical poetical themes to a rather bizarre level, one that seems to be conditioned by modern urban reality. Consequently his prose poems can be read as critical meta-commentaries to traditional poetry and as a *prosification* of traditional poetry.

Prosification: the general tendency of the modern development of poetry into so-called free verse. Traditional poetical signals, conditioned by metrics, rhythm and rhyme, became less important thus giving way to new strategies for providing language with poetical function. Some of these innovations were attributable to the simple fact that poetry was no longer an oral phenomenon but was written on paper for a page in a book: aural effects gave way to visual and spatial effects. This change may have historically been regarded as the succession of "natural" forms by artificial. In this sense, the development of poetry ran parallel to the modern development within music: from tonality into serial construction; and within visual art: from figuration into abstract form.

When I refer to this well-known development as "prosification" it is in order to adjust the perspective and to regard modern poetry in relation to prose (in the same way as Nietzsche wanted to regard good prose "*face to face with poetry*"). The famous definition of poetical function, as heightened attention to the linguistic expression (a definition first given by Roman Jacobson in the 1930s) is often regarded as ontological (as mentioned in chapter 3). In my view, this poetical attention is more a strategy than an essence. Indeed, a whole set of strategies that can all be related to prose. It is the "war" or interchange between poetry and prose that can take different forms, from open combat to peaceful coexistence.

Prosification affects not only traditional poetic forms, expressed in rhyme and rhythm, but also traditional poetical motifs and, not least, the subject that was regarded as the source for at least romantic poetry. A strong tendency in the modern poetry that I observe in the prose poem can be called reduction: the poetical subject is reduced, dethroned and dehumanized and attention is directed to language, to materiality, to things and to structures instead. An anecdotal prefiguration of this is given by Baudelaire in the prose poem, *Perte d'auréole*, describing how the poet has lost his traditional halo in the mud of the street – read: urban modernity.

He decides to go to the brothel instead of composing poetry in a more celestial setting. Prosaic materiality has been developed in many "thing-poems" during the 20th century, starting with Rilke's *Neue Gedichte* and continuing to great effect with William Carlos Williams' minimalistic poetry for instance and via Francis Ponge taking the side of things, *Le Parti Pris des Choses*. Versions of anti-subjective materiality are very much present in the poetry of today – it is certainly pertinent for the Mullen prose poem that I am about to read – and has developed into what is termed "language materiality". Its advocates suggest an imperative version of Mallarmé's famous recommendation from the essay "Crise de vers" (1895): to make the poetical subject disappear and to "delegate the initiative to the words."[56] The logical continuation of this position will probably be a digitalization of poetry, conditioned by the possibilities of electronic media. This new phase in the prosification of modern poetry and of the modern world can perhaps be glimpsed in the Mullen prose

---

56 "La disparition élocutoire du poète, qui cède l'initiative aux mots."

poem, although most certainly not in Tranströmer's. I shall therefore start my reading with Tranströmer.

*

Tomas Tranströmer's poems undergo a degree of development in the direction of prose in the sense that he favors a mixture of prose and poetry in his later collections (from the 1970s and 1980s). It is not simply a prosification; while he is using prose and prose poems, he is also cultivating rigorous and traditional poetical forms such as alcaic verse and haiku. This would indicate that his private "war" between poetry and prose does not take the form of open combat. Rather, he is trying to find peaceful forms of coexistence, with prose carrying poetry, commenting on poetry, interacting with poetry, instead of reducing poetry. As an example of this strategy, I have chosen the text "Madrigal" from the collection *For Living and Dead* (1989).

1. I inherited a dark wood where I seldom go. But
2. a day will come when the dead and the living trade places.
3. The wood will be set in motion. We are not without hope.
4. The most serious crimes will remain unsolved in spite of the efforts
5. of many policemen. In the same way there is somewhere in
6. our lives a great unsolved love. I inherited a dark
7. wood, but today I'm walking in the other wood, the light one.
8. All the living creatures that sing, wriggle, wag, and crawl!
9. It's spring and the air is very strong. I have graduated
10. from the university of oblivion and am as empty-handed as
11. the shirt on the clothesline
    (Translation: Robert Fulton)

The concluding metaphors of the two last lines are like poetical strokes of lightning at the end of the prose. Before that, the reader has been caught in simple oppositions: "the dark wood" from the beginning of the text is opposed to "the light one" (l. 7). The dead are opposed to the living (l. 2), perhaps in contrast to "all the living creatures" (l. 8. A more literal translation here is: "Everything living".) This symmetrical arrangement is, however, disturbed by the living and the dead trading places (l. 2) – an odd and disturbing movement, reminding you that the collection is called *For Living and Dead*. Neither is crime (l. 4) and love (l. 6) a solid opposition, since "hope" (l. 3) is related to crime as well as to love. Disturbances such as these install a kind of restlessness in a text that looks simple and compact at first sight; perhaps one could discern a poetical movement within the prose? This effect is emphasized by altering tenses: the preterite at the beginning quickly morphs into future tense and changes once more into present tense in l. 3 (A more literal translation here is: "Then the wood is set in motion.") The past, including unsolved crimes and loves, is associated with inheritance and darkness, the future holds a peculiar hope of the living and the dead trading places, the present is associated with light, spring and "everything living". Again, there are disturbances in this distribution: the interaction between the temporal levels undermines a stable opposition of the present versus the past. This interaction seems like a "courteous war" (in Nietzsche's terms) between poetry and prose. Yet the "war" is neither a polemical nor an aggressive one; instead one thinks of an ill-matched couple that has decided to continue to live together, after all. Alternatively, should one perhaps imagine poetry as wriggling out of the grip of prose? Perhaps the concluding metaphors announce liberation from the dark wood of prose?

Such constitutes the kind of existential reading that has dominated Swedish reception of this poetry. A prominent reader, Niklas Schiöler, writes that against the dark wood of the poem...

> ...including both good and evil, both past and future, stands the light wood, the here and now of lightness, the ecstatic forgetfulness outside history. Here, more than usual, Tranströmer approaches the ecstasy of self-abandon, extinguishing memory and emptying personality. The burden of time, inheritance, actions and sins of omission meet the ephemeral; 'today' is a state of exception. 'Today' is a euphoric, gracious now.

Schiöler associates the final metaphor – the empty-handed shirt – to the *via negativa* of classical mysticism, *showing* emptiness and demonstrating a "loophole to another and more gracious world."[57]

It is my opinion that this reading answers to the strong existential and perhaps "mystical" appeal of this text very well. Still, I would like to supplement it with some considerations on the relations to history and tradition. Such relations are suggested through the interaction between now and then in the text (allegorizing the interaction

---

57 Niklas Schiöler, *Koncentrationens konst. Tomas Tranströmers senare poesi*, Stockholm: Bonniers 1999, p. 147–149.

between poetry and prose). The immediate impression may very well be that the text commends liberation *from* the prose of both reality and history executed in the final lines: here, the strong presence of "today" interplays with the absence of the subject. The text is no doubt a variation on a theme of the mystics, a theme that has always been strong in Tranströmer's poetry, coordinated here with the reduction of the self that is prominent in modernism. (Although Tranströmer's existential version is quite different from what you find for instance in Ponge and in "language materialism".) However, the text reveals more possibilities. At the same time as it commends forgetfulness, it asks for liberation *through* history, an opening or clearing *in* the dark forest of history and tradition and social structure. It is the movements in the text, the trading of places and the shifting temporality, which open up this clearing. To phrase it in the words used in my point of departure: the text does not commend liberation from prose but aims for a mutually liberating interaction. This is no simple prosification, neither prose nor poetry, it is rather a poetically elevated prose, prose *face to face with poetry*.

In other words, the text may be read as being dominated by poetry as well as by prose (we are once more reminded of the title of the collection: for living as well as for dead). A first glance already admits both possibilities: if you are caught by the empty-handed shirt in the final line, you may *see* a liberated-liberating void. The reason is not solely that the shirt shows a reduction of humanity and subjectivity, but also that this line is the only irregular, shortened line. It operates like a poetical reminiscence ending in a void. If you, on the other hand, regard the text as a whole then you are met by a compact piece of prose, like a dark and almost impenetrable wood. When reading and discovering the temporal shifts and the suggestive trading of places, you are instead captivated by a movement that may lead you to a clearing *in* the text or *between* its lines.

I shall try do develop this meditation on poetry as prose into some considerations on poetry and history. Once more, I shall take my starting point as Nietzsche, this time in his second *Untimely Consideration: On the Uses and Disadvantage of History for Life* (1874). In this early work, Nietzsche famously discusses the tyranny of memory and history and our need for active forgetting. He pleads for something that Tranströmer's text also seems to commend: a break with the past in favor of the strong sense of living in the present. According to Nietzsche:

> He who cannot sink down on the threshold of the moment and forget all the past, who cannot stand balanced like a goddess of victory without growing dizzy and afraid, will never know what happiness is – [58]

A simple message: in the ecstatic moment of presence you should get rid of the burden of the past in order to enjoy "happiness". This figure of thought is no doubt close to our text in its poetical-mystical-existential version, when presence manifests itself in the "very strong" air of Spring culminating in the void of the last line. However, Nietzsche complicates his polemics with history by introducing an alternative and "critical" way of handling the burden of history. Now history itself is the answer to the problems of history: "history *must* itself resolve the problem of history, knowledge *must* turn its sting against itself." (*On the Uses*, p. 103) This kind of historical consciousness seems like a critical work *in* and *of* history. Furthermore, in this version history seems like a burden – a dark wood – but the task is not to get *out* of it but rather to get *into* it and find a way to carry the burden of history, to find some liberation *in* and *through* history.

There are indeed some opening movements in our text; some openings in the dark wood of history. The present tense of the text invites us (in l. 8) to an opening of "everything living", and the ardently piled verbs tell us about elementary activity and movement. Likewise, Nietzsche's liberating strategies aim at "everything living", as one could see from the quotation above appealing to the "moment of the threshold ". Perhaps there is a contradiction here between a prosaic and a poetical version of the text? Seeking liberation *in* and *through* the prosaic text means looking for the clearing that is the space for "everything living". The poetic version, on the other hand, culminates in a void that provides liberation from both the prose of history and also from *life*. Both readings agree, however, that the text is aiming for a kind of liberation: from, to, in or through life.

Tranströmer does not advocate any liberating means, of course; he is strictly descriptive, sketching liberation as a movement in time, as a change in pace and tense. In l. 8, he is creating an acceleration of "everything living" that prepares the "loophole" of the final line and its leap out of history – alternatively he could simply be offering a version of the mobility and change that *is* and *makes* life and history. I shall try to develop this possibility via association with the famous

---

58 Transl. R. J: Hollingdale, Cambridge University Press, 1997. Reference will be given in the text.

lines used by Hölderlin in order to conclude a stanza in *his* poem on memory and forgetting, *Mnemosyne*:

> ... Lang ist
> Die Zeit, es ereignet sich aber
> Das Wahre.
>
> ("--- Though the time / Be long, truth / Will come to pass.")
> *(Transl. Richard Sieburth)*

Let us imagine "history" as the kind of time that Hölderlin calls "long": this is the continuous and continuing time that Hölderlin describes in heavily falling syllables, the extension of the dactyl ("Lang ist") being emphasized by the shift of lines. After the solemn naming of the long time of history comes a caesura, concentrated to the comma of the second line quoted. The event that takes place after the caesura – the event that is "the true" – interrupts the extended fall of history in a violently rising rhythm. Two anapaests make way for the truth of the final line, which levels the conflicting rhythmical movements with equal stress on both syllables of the truth ("Das Wahre"). One perhaps could say, as with Nietzsche, that history itself as a momentary event dissolves the problem of history as tradition and inheritance, as time falling. Hölderlin makes the lapse of time unite with the event in time; such is "the true" of his poem of memory. (Should I venture to relate this speculation to my discussion on poetry and prose, I could say that the poetical event breaks the prose of history while the prose poem is uniting both.)

Hölderlin says nothing of the contents of this rhythmical drama, besides historical time being "long", nor does he indicate how the dramatic change into "the true" comes about. Neither does Tranströmer give any directions for his prosaic history but he, as Hölderlin, describes its events like rhythmical shifts, not far from Hölderlin's dramatic change of pace. The dark wood from the first line of our text shifts to acceleration: "But a day will come" (more efficient in the original). When the dark wood returns (l. 6–7), it is immediately countered by a new defiant anapaest: "But today". These shifts of pace, that are also shifts of tense, *open* the text. The first time into the foreboding of the day "when the dead and the living trade places" – sounding ominous as well as promising. (Does this mean that the border between living and dead is sustained or erased?) The second time, we are invited to the "light wood" containing "everything living". "The true", in Hölderlin's *Mnemosyne*, was a tense unity of the lapse of time with the temporal event. "Everything living" in Tranströmer's text is the life to be lived when checking yourself on what Nietzsche called the "threshold of the moment". Alternatively, this strong appeal to presence is perhaps merely a preparation for the mysterious disappearance that takes place in the last lines of our text?

I am unable to choose between these alternatives (I am not even sure that they are alternatives). Instead, I want to broaden the perspective into a couple of other directions. Thus far, I have associated the dark wood of our text with prose and history. Yet an allegorizing reading can take many other directions. Why not a psychological one? Imagine the dark and the light wood as a metaphorical construction of the very Self that is to be reduced! Imagine the changes of pace as descriptions of the interchange between inherited darkness (crime, love!) with the light of presence and consciousness! In that case, my two alternatives, or overlapping readings, consist of the loophole of constriction and repression competing with the clearing of therapy ... Why not philosophically? The dark wood as the collected metaphysical thinking of the West, the light wood as the event – Heidegger's clearing in his *Schwarzwald* – which emits a moment of truth in our darkness? Why not poetologically, with the "I" of the text as the Poet of today, wrestling with tradition as well as presence? The many literary hints of the text support a poetological reading. There are associations with both other parts of Tranströmer's poetical universe and also with world literature: the place-trading of "the dead and the living" directs us to the title of the collection, but also imparts a taste of Ibsen's last play (*When We Dead Awaken*) and possibly prepares the relation to *Macbeth*, that becomes evident in l. 3, when "the wood will be set in motion." The dark wood of our text not only signals Birnam's wood but possibly Baudelaires forest of symbols too, and, of course, Dante's *selva oscura* – with Dante the "I" of our text makes a journey from darkness into light. Perhaps the wood of our text, dark as well as light, signifies "literature" – since Vergil's *silvae* meant poetical forest and later came to symbolize "books".

This is not to say that I am able to infer any obvious meaning out of the world-literary associations that I have accumulated (I am sure that there is more to be found). No doubt, our text can be read without literature so to speak (as well as without psychology and philosophy). None of my associations provide a "key" with which to open the compact, well-sealed text (nor does the title *Madrigal*). Perhaps the literary associations can help our treatment of the dark wood of the text as inheritance, tradition and prosaic history, however. I believe that the literary associations confirm the movement leading *into* the woods of the text, rather than *out* of it. The text culminates in oblivion and disappearance. However, the text also takes us back and commends a work of tradition: at the "university of oblivion" we learn that history itself must "dissolve the problem of history". This means that we read an alternative to the de-humanizing version of prosification common in modern prosified poetry. Instead, Tranströmer asks us to enter the forest of prose in order to uncover the openings of poetry, bringing prose and poetry into interplay. The prose-poem implodes the traditional poem, compressing it into a compact block of prose. The prose-poem may seem to have forgotten, or perhaps hidden, its poetry; nevertheless, the poetry is revealed in the restless movements of the text. Tranströmer's prose-poem does not abandon; it shows prose working with poetry, being written from the perspective of poetry.

*

The modern prosification of poetry cooperates with a reductive and de-humanizing tendency that is fatal for traditional as well as Romantic views of the poetical subject. Tranströmer's text, as discussed above, demonstrates this tendency at the same time as undermining it. As mentioned in the beginning of this chapter, the reductive version has a lineage that goes back to Mallarmé, expanding into different contemporary versions of "language materialism". One could perhaps say that de-humanized poetry gives an adequate expression of a de-humanized society, or a critical view of such a society. In either case, we have a prosified language showing us a state of prose – unfortunately one far away from the messianic state that Benjamin evoked as "universal history" and called prose (as discussed in chapter 4). Still, there may be glimpses of poetry as well as humanity in utterly materialistic prose. Close scrutiny of Francis Ponge's poems would no doubt reveal a few glimpses of this, even in his most deadpan prosaic poems. I will however take a contemporary example from the Afro-American writer, Harryette Mullen, a distinguished poet on the frontline of prosified poetry.[59] Here is a page from *Sleeping with the Dictionary* (2002):

Elliptical

They just can't seem to ... They should try harder to ... They ought to be more ... We all wish they weren't so ... They never ... They always ... Sometimes they ... Once in a while they ... However it is obvious that they ... Their overall tendency has been ... The consequences of which have been ... They don't appear to understand that ... If only they would make an effort to ... But we know how difficult it is for them to ... Many of them remain unaware of ... Some who should know better simply refuse to ... Of course, their perspective has been limited by ... On the other hand, they obviously feel entitled to ... Certainly we can't forget that they ... Nor can it be denied that they ... We know that this has had an enormous impact on their ... Nevertheless their behaviour strikes us as ... Our interactions unfortunately have been ...

The title "Elliptical" refers to the many incomplete sentences that are piled up here in order to form a kind of a "poem". The sentences – or the fragments of sentences – are separated by the three dots, these in themselves make up a series of ellipses. The dots are a graphic arrangement, made for the book-page; dots have no equivalent in spoken language except for pauses and silence. The sentences (or fragments) are separated at the same time as being connected by the three dots, this can therefore be seen as a gesture of prose: the dots signal contingency while they still make connections alluding to a lost or never found coherence and closure.

The sentences that are separated (while still connected) by the three dots seem to be drawn out of a meeting of sorts, emanating from several voices engaged in discussion. They seem to discuss what could be a drop-out case or a football team or a research group, for instance. Whichever kind of phenomenon they are discussing probably does not matter very much: the interesting feature is that a discussion is taking place and that the poem gives a fragmentary account of this. We can sense a development in the discussion: the fragments express disappointment and despite some lines, which look like sympathetic objections ("On the other hand"), the final

---

59 I am reusing and expanding the analysis of this poem in the chapter "Prose" in *Aesthetics at Work* (my edition), Oslo: Unipub 2007.

ellipse probably states that the discussion will end in an unfavorable conclusion for the person, object or association under discussion.

The poem therefore seems to represent a predominantly prosaic situation, taken for instance from a meeting room of a social welfare office. This meeting discusses a very prosaic reality, the negative conduct of a client, for example. The conclusion (if there is to be a conclusion) will surely be just as prosaic. However, we must guess at the contents of the discussion and the conclusion can only be inferred by extension of the text. The poem states nothing. Instead, it is attending the voices, or perhaps the sentences, as they are rendered in ellipses and fragments. The poem seems to be *overheard*: the poem has been substituted via a receiver that happens to register voices (or bits of voices). These voices/sentences are marked by contingency in several ways: we get the impression that the choice of voices is randomly made and is just as arbitrary at the beginning of the text as at the end. The sentences are fragmentary, implying that the receiver has only managed to register accidental portions of what was said. The voices and the sentences could just as well continue. The voices are furthermore demonstratively anti-poetical: they express themselves trivially and prosaically concerning a trivial and prosaic situation. There is no poetical subject to be found that can grant us with meaning or even expression.

This is a stark contrast to Tranströmer's text. There, we felt that each word was necessary and the whole was composed with equal necessity, just like a good, old poem. In Mullen's text, nothing seems necessary. There is no progress (or hardly any progress), indicating that the order of the ellipses could equally be quite different and that any of the fragments could be either dropped or exchanged with another. Anything and everything is replaceable and interchangeable. Indeed, that may well be the very point of the text: to demonstrate complete contingency, a state that is elliptical in the sense that there is no closure, no inherent structure and meaning.

Perhaps we can say that Mullen gives a radical version of Mallarmé's recommendation: to "delegate the initiative to the words" while disappearing as an instituting subject. (Again, that disappearance is something other than the mystical emptying performed by Tranströmer.) The words are given initiative in the sense that we read what an apparently neutral receiver has registered in a seemingly haphazard order. The language as a machine has produced a text parading as a poem. Such a reading has to be modified in at least two ways, however:

Firstly, the text may be read as a poetical intervention, with elements of poetry breaking into this prosaic chatter through interrupting the sentences and arranging the fragments into a pattern with rhythmical qualities, thereby transforming the elliptical sentences into something similar to breath. The absent poet listens on our behalf and discreetly arranges what she hears in such a way as to help us notice the cruelly prosaic character of the situation – as well as its poetical possibilities. Even the most prosaic of languages is always on the verge of poetry. Furthermore, our elliptical text reminds us that the prosaic poetry of reduction encourages other qualities than the traditionally lyrical, such as visual and even performative qualities for instance. The many dots of the text function as linguistic gestures rather than signs, performing the elliptical state that the poem itself is all about.

Secondly, this text gives a preview of what may well be the next stage in the prosification of poetry: its digitalization. Electronics has imparted new possibilities to developing a text, that the interacting reader constructs as a poem. The poet as programmer! The visual workings in prosified poetry are, of course, given a new dimension with novel graphic design possibilities. In a debate from 1892 on photographic pictures in literary texts, Mallarmé is said to have welcomed such an invention. He was even looking forward to the day when mobile pictures could enrich the graphics of literature.[60] Well, this became possible some hundred years later and today is employed as the graphic design of the computerized "page" in digitalized poetry.

Mullen's text is clearly not digitalized in any technical sense. Regardless of this, it enacts some of the possibilities of digitalization: the visual arrangement, the replaceability of its sentences, the performative potential. Its reduction of the traditional poetical subject has made us ask whether the initiative may be delegated to language itself. The association to digitalized poetry makes the way for a further question: Is the initiative handed over to the reader?

Perhaps Walter Benjamin's "distracted" but still "discerning" viewer – as presented in chapter 3 – has finally found his medium when

---

60 According to the commentary in Georges Rodenbach, *Bruges-la-mort*, Paris: Flammarion 1998.

sitting in front of the screen and interacting with poetical possibilities? Perhaps this situation presents a new stage in the prosification of language and reality? The web may be world-wide but it is still far away from the "universal history" that Benjamin expected as prose. Still, it must be admitted that the prose of the computer opens up some new possibilities for poetry. The last fragment of Mullen's text – "Our interactions unfortunately have been …" – may not be the last word. In a digitalized world, there are no last words. Fortunate interactions are always possible.

III Prose on the Borderlines of Fiction

Sightseeing: Travel Writing

In this chapter, I investigate the prose of modern travel writing. The idea: travel writers present poignant versions of modern prose – prose moving beyond the fictional borders. I shall make my case with the help of the Norwegian writers Cora Sandel and Åsne Seierstad; furthermore, I shall use some modern classics in travel writing: Robert Byron, Nicolas Bouvier, Ryszard Kapuściński, V. S. Naipaul and Elias Canetti. They present different versions of a common project: *learning to see.* Also, learning to write a new kind of prose.

Travel writing between fact and fiction

Travel writing is difficult to situate within the literary tradition and in modern literature. Travel writing seems to be at once both prominent and peripheral. This ambiguous position no doubt depends on the traveler's application of discourses of uncertain literary status such as journalistic reporting and biography. Traveling has of course always been important in literature, as a motif and a motor. I hardly need to remind the reader that the travelogue of Ulysses constitutes one of the first epics of Western literature. Dante's travel through Inferno to Paradise was the first great imaginary and metaphysical voyage. The novel, in the modern sense of the word, was born when Cervantes had his anonymous petty nobleman adopt the name Don Quijote and hit the road. Defoe contributed to the constitution of the modern individual when his Crusoe set foot off the boat. No doubt: great literary inventions are motivated by travels.

Still, travel writing occupies no obvious or "natural" place within literary history and criticism, not even within what we acknowledge as "literature." The critic, along with the average reader, the librarian and the bookseller has difficulty deciding whether travel writing is a special branch of literature or whether it belongs even to literature in a general sense of the word. There is, according to Michael Kowaleski in his introduction to an anthology on travel writing, "a venerable tradition of condescending to travel-books as a secondary-rate literary form."[61] Paul Fussell, who wrote an entertaining book on English travel writing between the wars, blames the romantic myth of creation for this:

> The genres with current prestige are the novel and the lyric poem although it does not seem to matter that very few memorable examples of either ever appear. The status of those two kinds is largely an unearned and unexamined snob increment from late-romantic theories of imaginative art as religion-cum-metaphysics. Other kinds of works – those relegated to simple-minded categories like 'the literature of fact' or 'the literature of argument' are in lower esteem artistically because the term *creative* has been widely misunderstood, enabling its votaries to vest it with magical powers. Before that word had been promoted to the highest esteem, that is, before the Romantic movement, a masterpiece was conceivable in a 'non-fictional' genre like historiography or memoir or the long essay or biography or the travel book.[62]

What Fussell calls *literature of fact* cannot be called literature should the idea of literature be occupied exclusively by "fiction", and limited to the novel, poetry and drama. Travel writing is often both — it insists on being factual and truthful while using elements of fiction at the same time. Travel writing is prose that can approach fiction and go beyond fiction yet also dwell in poetry.

I will, however, devote a few words to the complication concerning the opposition fact/fiction and its relevance for travel writing. The reason is simple: the traveler uses literary devices to make his story readable. And the literary technique makes (or *can* make) the truthfulness of the story debatable. The fact is, that the narrator and the position of the narrator are rarely exposed in travel writing (in contrast to novelistic writing) — we do not expect unreliable narrators in travel writing. Instead, the narrator presents himself as for instance a *witness*, who really has seen and experienced the reality they tells us about. But the position of the witness also (and therefore the reliability of his story) calls for literature to be established.

An example of this is when Primo Levi in *La Tregua* (1963, *The Truce*) related his near-year-long journey transporting him, along

---

[61] "Introduction: The Modern Literature of Travel", in *Temperamental Journeys. Essays on the Modern Literature of Travel*, University of Georgia Press 1992, p. 2.
[62] *Abroad. British Literary Travelling Between the Wars*, Oxford University Press, 1980, p. 213.

with other camp-prisoners in 1945 from Auschwitz to Belorussia, Romania, Hungary and Austria, before he finally returns to Turin. He tells us about this in an artless and matter-of-fact manner. He does not even evoke the present tense to emphasize that he was there. In the earlier book *Se questo è un uomo* (1947, *If This is a Man*) he gives us one of the most famous narrations from a concentration camp, unsurpassed in its detailed factuality. There, he tends to use the present tense to stress his position as a witness: not only "I was there" but even *I am here*. His travelogue instead has the character of a picaresque novel, where bizarre, touching and sometimes entertaining episodes follow each other along the traveler's road. Even if Levi does not use the present tense here, he often uses direct speech to imbue his episodes with a visual dimension and presence.

Present tense and direct speech are fictional devices frequently used in modern travel writing. The writer wants to give the impression of an immediate presence: he presents himself as in the middle of the journey handing over the position of the witness to us, the readers. Strikingly, many travel books are construed as journals or logbooks. Still, there is clearly a temporal distance between the travel and the writing and the travel writer uses literary technique when handling this distance. Some simulate the conjunction of narration and event while others can use the same artifice playfully: "Enough of this for the moment" exclaims Robert Byron in *The Road to Oxiana*[63] pretending that he is slamming the book shut — the diary — that we are supposedly reading. Others can emphasize and thereby take advantage of the distance between event and writing, "But then why insist on talking about this journey?" Nicolas Bouvier asks himself. "What bearing does it have on my life at present? None; anyway, I no longer have a present."[64] This comes from an italicized passage toward the end of his great travel book from Asia, *The Way of the World (L'usage du monde* 1963), a notice headed "Six years later". Elias Canetti gave his travel book from Morocco, *The voices of Marrakesh (Die Stimmen von Marrakesch* 1967) the subtitle "Notes after a journey" – an innocent but efficient emphasis of the fact that writing necessarily takes place *after* the event.[65] Patrick Leigh Fermor has

---

63   Robert Byron, *The Road to Oxiana*, Penguin 1992 (1937), p. 96.
64   Nicolas Bouvier, *The Way of the World*, transl. Robyn Marsack, Marlboro Press 1992, p. 299. Pages will be given in the text.
65   The subtitle has been dropped in the English translation by J. A. Underwood, London: Marion Boyars 1993 (1982). Pages will be given in the text.

a distance of forty to fifty years when he records his story of walking through Europe in the 1930s (*A Time of Gifts* 1977, *Between the Woods and the Water* 1986); he occasionally quotes a juvenile diary but most often has his young persona adopt the perspective of the elderly man.

One of my favorite travelers of today is the Polish writer Ryszard Kapuściński. In his book, from the decaying Soviet Union (*Imperium* 1993) he extensively uses devices such as the present tense, direct speech as well as *style indirect libre* meaning his narration is colored by the language of the other. An example of this comes in Turkmenistan. Kapuściński gives the word to a figure he calls "the old man" while keeping his presentation in the third person: "He knows what thirst is and how it feels to have one's thirst quenched." And: "He has seen the desert, and he has seen the oasis, and in the final analysis it comes down to this one division."[66] Who is talking in phrases like that: Kapuściński or the "old one"? The problem (if it is a problem) is well known in the history of the novel: Flaubert used this technique extensively, making it difficult for the reader to distinguish Madame Bovary from her narrator. In Flaubert's case one could perhaps talk of *fictionalization*, while Kapuściński wants to install a persuasive presence. The conclusion must be that credibility is produced by literary and rhetorical artifice. Truth is not (or not only) a question of the correspondence between historic reality and its presentation. Truth has to be produced.

Kapuściński demonstrates what could resemble a paradox: credibility demands literary construction. Although fiction seems contrary to reality, fictional device is used in the presentation and construction of reality; such is the condition of modern prose. Other travel writers make more use than Kapuściński does of fiction; while others "factualize" to persuade us that they are telling the very truth about reality, exactly as it was and is.

The documentary and factual effect is also an effect that has to be produced. Visual media of today have accustomed us to the hidden camera, documentaries arrange their documentation, news programs can make the simplest news-flash look like a reality "soap" while "soaps" try to look like news programs. We meet the same tendency in the travel writing of today, for instance the Norwegian writer

---

66   *Imperium*, transl. Klara Glowczewska, New York: Knopf 1994, p. 61. Pages will be given in the text.

Åsne Seierstad's *The Bookseller of Kabul*. Seiersted transforms herself to a hidden camera and avoids all that could remind the reader of her actual writing. Direct speech and the present tense dominate: "I am seventeen, he thinks. Life is over before it has even started."[67] The present tense indicates that the narrator's interpretation of the situation ("life is over") is not to be taken as an interpretation, and not as a quotation, but instead as coming directly out of the head of the person. The presentation wishes to be met as authentically real, as a document. This is not a question of the fictional declaration "all similarity with reality is coincidental" but of the documentary declaration: "this is a true story".

Both Kapuściński and Seierstad use literary artifice to produce credibility and it would be preposterous to say that one method is inherently better than the other. I am therefore tempted to side with Nietzsche in a conclusion to this short discussion of fiction and fact in travel writing. I am thinking here of the epistemological perspectivism offered in *On the Genealogy of Morality*: "There is *only* a perspective seeing, *only* a perspective 'knowing' /.../ the *more* eyes, various eyes we are able to use for the same thing, the more complete will be our 'concept' of the thing, our 'objectivity'."[68]

Mapping, seeing, meeting

Truth and credibility of travel writing depend on the perspective used by the narrator to present/represent travel in writing, to translate/transform travel into writing. Such was the conclusion that I now want to progress to a review of current perspectives in travel writing, thus preparing the ground for a procession of seven literary examples, all with their own strategies for the prose of sightseeing.

The dependence of truth on perspective of course goes beyond modern travel writing: perhaps as far back as to the beginning! I am thinking of Herodotus: his histories from the fourth century BC make him the "father" of travel writing, the "father" of History and perhaps also to the "father" of the recurrent idea of a clash between the civilizations of East and West. The French philologist François

---

67 Åsne Seierstad, *The Bookseller of Kabul*, transl. Ingrid Christophersen, Virago 2004, p. 132. Pages will be given in the text.
68 Transl. R.J. Hollingdale. In *The Nietzsche Reader*, ed. Keith Ansell Pearson & Duncan Large, Blackwell 2006, p. 427.

Hartog has observed that Herodotus "translates" what seemed different, *l'alterité*, into the well known, into his own domain. His rhetorical strategy is to make the foreign cultures he tells us about conceivable and understandable for himself and for his readers/listeners using his own culture as the norm of understanding. The other and foreign culture is a version of his own, a deviation or an opposition; it can be *compared* to his own and, in the best instances, show signs of *analogy* of his own. The strategy most often used by Herodotus is, according to Hartog, the *inversion*: he simply presents the other culture as the opposite of his own. Thus either what his own culture is not or his own culture turned upside down. The inversion is a "convenient" strategy according to Hartog. It makes the other, and other-ness, into the opposite of your own and therefore "transparent" – entirely possible to understand – for the reader/listener: "there is no longer an *a* and *b*, but simply an *a* and the inversion of *a*."[69] The first and decisive artifice of travel writing: it tells us about the Other but at the same time makes the Other disappear *as* the Other by transforming it into your own (or to the flipside of your own).

I am not sure if Hartog's observations do Herodotus full justice, but I must admit that they are still poignant. They are certainly relevant according to the critics of travel writing, especially the English-writing critics that have been inspired by Foucault's analysis of power in combination with Edward Said's *Orientalism* (1978). What is the very arena of modern travel writing — the meeting of the traveler with the foreign other — if it is not a scene where the traveler exercises power in relation to the Other? Travel writers deal with *mapping*, according to Dennis Porter: "they are engaged in a form of cultural cartography that is impelled by an anxiety to map the globe, center it on a certain point, produce explanatory narratives, and assign fixed identities to regions and the races that inhabit them."[70] Patrick Holland and Graham Huggan add that, such *mapping* "frequently provides an effective alibi for the perpetuation or reinstallment of ethnocentrically superior attitudes to 'other' cultures,

---

69 François Hartog, *Le miroir d'Hérodote. Essai sur la représentation de l'autre*. Paris: Gallimard 1980, p. 225f.
70 Dennis Porter: *Haunted Journeys. Desire and Transgression in European Travel Writing*. Princeton University Press, 1991, p. 20.

peoples, and places."[71] Mary Louise Pratt, in her ruthless analysis of travel writing, describes the ideological consequences of *mapping* as the writer exercising "a discourse of negation, domination, devaluation , and fear that remains in the late twentieth century a powerful ideological constituent of the West's consciousness of the people and places it strives to hold in subjugation."[72]

Mapping is certainly a suggestive term in this setting. It connects directly to what was an important ingredient in travel writing, at least from Marco Polo onwards: naming "unknown" territory, making way for further orientation and for physical exploitation. In a broader sense of the term, *mapping* suggests what Pratt had in mind when she named her book *Imperial Eyes*: the gaze used by the traveler in order to register, examine and organize the reality they meet, to make the strange and foreign less strange and if not well known, then at least possible to survey and understand. In an even broader sense, one can think of the term *mapping* as describing the very normal and everyday activity of the eye when it receives its visual impressions and organizes them to make sense and order in the chaotic world of forms and colors. *Mapping* is therefore a useful concept when it comes to describing the strategy of the traveler in their representation of foreign reality. *Mapping* is even useful as a description of the strategies of modern *prose*. Furthermore, *mapping* has become part of the vocabulary of cognitive psychology, when it comes to describing our remarkable capacity for inventing *metaphors* to make reality conceivable. Perhaps travel writing could be regarded as an extended metaphorical activity? Perhaps *mapping* is a version of the capacity Nietzsche called *interpretation* and honored as our most important tool as we make our way in the world and try to gain "power" over our perceptions and thereby over reality. We remember that Nietzsche recommended "perspectivism" when approaching reality with the motivation that reality, according to him, does not consist of neutral "facts" but instead depends on the subjectivity that "interprets" using "perspective."

Is *mapping* a good term when it comes to describing the rhetorical strategy of the modern travel writer? I have to oppose the

---

71 Patrick Holland & Graham Huggan: *Tourists with Typewriters. Critical Reflections on Contemporary Travel Writing*. Michigan University Press, 1998, p. viii.
72 Mary Louise Pratt: *Imperial Eyes. Travel Writing and Transculturation*, London: Routledge 1992, p. 219.

critics mentioned above and announce my doubt, at this point. As a phenomenological concept, *mapping* is always useful in describing the relation between myself and the world. If we pull the term in Nietzsche's direction, one could even maintain that the travelogue is a kind of allegory over the interpretative perspective(s) used by my approach to reality. The elements of the travel story — someone traveling into what is foreign to them, meeting a world, trying to find their way in the unknown, trying to understand — give an archaic model for *any* human meeting with the world – not least in the versions of modern prose. But that is not the same as saying that travel writing is using imperialistic techniques for domination. I think we have every reason to read much travel writing from the 18th and 19th centuries as mapping contributions to imperialism. Mapping in the concrete sense of charting and surveying and naming is also given a space that strikes a modern reader as beyond reason and even comical. If I point to a modern turn of this, then I find it in the transition from Henry Stanley's *In Darkest Africa* (1890) — a travel story explicitly mapping "white patches" — into Joseph Conrad's *Heart of Darkness* (1900) where the "white patch" has become a location of darkness (as Conrad puts it in his Congo diary).

Conrad has, of course, made fiction out of his travel story, he has erased the geographical contours and his traveler has become what Stanley and exploiting travelers before him, seldom were: hesitating, critical, self-conscious. If there had earlier been a relation of power between the norm(ality) of the traveler and the inversion or deviation of the foreign, this is substituted for *interaction* by Conrad. By this I mean an exchange between the subject and the foreign other which also presupposes unknown depths within the subject, inferring that the supposedly well known is also fundamentally unknown. *Mapping* becomes *meeting*.

The meeting can, of course, take many forms, including versions of power. I will now delimit myself to exploring those forms and versions that can be described as *visual strategies* in travel writing. Every traveler must learn to see. The tourist with the camera to his eye reminds us that the traveler wants to safeguard what he sees and that he must slow down and stop when seeing a sight, choose perspective, focus. Slowing down, coming to a halt, seems to be the first and necessary step to take in when you really want to see. The fact that you have to stand still to use the camera is a practical as well as symbolical demonstration of the demands of seeing. It comes close to a dilemma that faces anyone visiting a museum of art: you have to pass through the collection and see as much as possible but you also have to slow down and stop to really see the single work. *Learning to see* is the task and the first lesson to learn is to slow down; if you want to document your journey you have to freeze it. If you want to make your journey into literature you have to interrupt it and make space for the distance and perspective demanded by writing.

The art of seeing has strong philosophical implications and traditions and the task — *learning to see* — is not restricted to travelers or museum-visitors. It must be called a phenomenological challenge connected to the understanding and handling of our life world. The philosopher treating seeing as a project is also the godfather of modern phenomenology: Nietzsche. In his late work, *The Twilight of the Idols* he reaches the conclusion that seeing things *as they are* implies slowing down, resisting hasty judgments, "suspending the decision":

> *Learning to see*, as I understand it, is close to what an unphilosophical way of speaking calls a strong will: the essential thing here is precisely *not* 'to will', to be *able* to suspend the decision.[73]

This declaration on the phenomenology of seeing seems like a lesson for those modern travelers, that allow themselves to be more interested in meeting than mapping, more interested in seeing than in sights. Nietzsche was a nomadic thinker moving as restlessly in his mind as in the European geography: without a domicile, without a homeland ... insisting that good thinking demands the use of your feet and that sitting still is the greatest sin ... I therefore permit myself to evoke Nietzsche as a guardian angel in this review of some literary strategies of sightseeing.

*

Cora Sandel is a pen name for Sara Fabricius. She left Norway for Paris as a young woman at the beginning of the 20th century to become a painter, and returned as a writer in the 1920s. She is best known for her novel-trilogy on Alberta, the first part presents Alberta growing up in northern Norway; the second part, Alberta in Paris; and the third, Alberta on her way back to Norway. I am concentrating here

---

[73] Transl. Judith Norman. In Nietzsche, *The Anti-Christ, Ecce Homo, Twilight of the Idols And Other Writings*. Cambridge University Press, 2005, p. 190.

on the second of these novels, *Alberta and Freedom*, first published in 1931, and I am reading it as a kind of travelogue contained within the three-part novel of development. It gives us a remarkable version of a grand theme: the Northerner meeting the South. Here is the young and inexperienced Northern woman coming to Paris, the city where you expect to experience modernity in art and living. Paris: a site for modernization and transformation. The novel is modern travel writing in several senses of the term: Sandel's Alberta is a city nomad, contemporary with for instance Woolf's *Mrs. Dalloway*, Djuna Barnes' heroines of the *Nightwood*, Louis Aragon's *Paysan de Paris*. Like these, Alberta spends much of her time *walking* the streets and Sandel equips her with an "inclination to drift."[74] Alberta has traveled away (from Norway) and she will travel back again (although she does not know) but in Paris she travels on the spot. Her journey comes to a stop in Paris and she seems to have no aim for being there other than being there, lingering there; waiting for something to happen. This combination of stop-lingering-waiting and restless street- drifting is used to characterizing Alberta's life situation, her social and erotic contacts. It also characterizes her hesitating efforts to become a writer. I will however restrict myself to an example of her *seeing*. Through Alberta Cora Sandel develops a visual capacity that I consider to be an important part of the modernism of her novel: Sandel aims at seeing things as they are and seeing reality in a new way. Without employing the terminology, she joins the program expressed at her time in early modernism — more explicitly in cubism, futurism, suprematism and surrealism — programs inherited from the task that Nietzsche called *learning to see*.

Sandel's school of seeing is a consequence of her slowing down. She makes Alberta stay in the Parisian moment while waiting for something to happen. The narrator joins Alberta in a common project that could be called an aesthetics-in-waiting, breaking up the narrative pulse and teleology into visual scenes. Sandel frequently uses one, two and three dashes to install a panting rhythm in the text, an illusion of a restless and repeated Now as a text-version of Alberta's nomadic "drifting" in the streets of Paris. (Unfortunately much of this effect has disappeared from the English translation.) An excellent example is a scene from a painter's study (p. 46ff.), a scene used

---

74 Transl. Elizabeth Rokkan, Peter Owen 1963, p. 42. Pages will be given in the text.

to discuss and illustrate the conditions of seeing. We are invited to observe what is going on through the eyes of Alberta while informed that she does not want to be seen: "Across a muddled still life of bottles, glasses, fruit peelings and ashtrays Alberta defended herself through the tobacco smoke against several pair of eyes." These intruding eyes belong to different young men who are all interested in Alberta (whom is single), while Alberta "defends herself" since the men would threaten her nomadic project by forcing her to make a decision and commit herself. The scene is inhabited by at least ten people with at least six nationalities. These are profiled both visually and linguistically with fragments in French, Swedish, Danish, English and German punctuating the Norwegian language of the narration. But the Norwegian is also stylized and transformed into poetical material: "Alberta had gradually come to hear Norwegian from the outside." She (and therefore we) does not hear it as narration or communication but as sound: "It can sound musical, being securely embedded in a light, strong, slightly differentiated register and having its own clear staccato melody. It is without evasion, going directly to the point, an honest, forthright language." In agitated conversation, it is different: "the brief sentences, the disconnected, self-sufficient words dart at each other like angry barks." Sandel thus uses the privilege of the travel writer as well as the exiled writer: directing a critical gaze to the origin and to oneself.

Cubism serves as a theme for the discussion in this scene, being highly topical at the time of the novel and leading us to Sandel's aesthetics. The scene starts visually in an impressionistic mode — the detached remarks, the visual and linguistic fragments — but develops into a kind of cubism: the sights and regards and the languages are stopped in the moment, cut up into smaller units that are attached to each other and against each other in rhythmical combinations and relations.

There is, of course, much more to be said about Sandel's elegant handling of visual and auditory effects: having Alberta act as a nude model introduces a strong visual theme with many implications; although I shall stop here because I believe I have made my point. Sandel interrupts a traditional epic narration — the novel of development — and transforms it into a prose that comes close to visual poetry. She installs a tension between epic movement, epic teleology and poetical spatiality in her text, a tension well known to modernist classics. This tension also has something to tell us about the possibilities of travel writing. The epic position reminds us of the tourist, who plans his traveling and knows how to get back, who works to *map* things and reality, who wants to capture, collect and order his *sights*. But there is also another kind of traveler, who is willing to linger, to pause and to make the foreign reality speak for itself. This lingering traveler resists from passing judgment; he suspends his decisions. He is learning to see.

*

Robert Byron travels from Venice through Palestine to Persia and Afghanistan before going back to England via India. This is the beginning of the 1930s; Byron travels for eleven months and it takes several years for him to formulate his impressions into the book that was published in 1937: *The Road to Oxiana*. I have already mentioned that Byron uses diary form, direct speech and the present tense to give the impression of presence. Still, his prime faculty when it comes to writing is his memory.

Byron's driving force was to find and describe the foremost examples of Islamic architecture and decorative art, especially mosaic. Furthermore he wanted to reach the river Oxus (now the Amu Darya river), a Turcmen-uzbec river, once marking the borderline between the oldest civilizations of the world and the nomads of Central Asia. Despite fighting all sorts of bureaucratic and practical obstacles, Byron still does not manage to get a permit to go where he wants to go. Although he at least reaches the steppe of Turcmenistan:

> Suddenly, as a ship leaves an estuary, we came out on to the steppe: a dazzling open sea of green. I never saw that color before. /.../ This was the pure essence of green, indissoluble, the color of life itself. The sun was warm, the larks were singing up above. Behind us rose the misty Alpine blue of the wooded Elburz. In front, the glowing verdure stretched out to the rim of the earth. (P. 227f.)

The quotation would show that Byron relates his visual impressions as revelations, as epiphanies, as *sights*, that flash through the otherwise ironically described nuisances of his journey. It is primarily when confronted with good art that visual impressions are permitted to overwhelm the traveler and most of all in the culminating experience of the book: a visit to Meshed in the North East of Iran. There he locates a temple built by Gohar Shad, a medieval ruler — a woman! — and, according to Byron, one of the greatest master builders of all time. The problem is that the unfaithful are not permitted to approach the inner building and this provokes a wittily related conspiracy from Byron. Finally, he dresses like an Arab and slips in:

> I invented a quick Persian-looking trot of short high steps that would prevent me from tripping over uneven paving-stones; but no one looked at me. The goal grew nearer. There was the main gate. There the little tunnel. Without looking round I was in it, found the yard, realized there were trees there, and then saw that the further exit was completely blocked by a group of mullahs, my potential assaulters, /.../ I hastened down the dark bazaar, found the dome where I turned to the left, and was greeted, on coming out into the court, by such a fanfare of color and light that I stopped a moment, half blinded. It was as if someone had switched on another sun. (P. 243)

Byron prepares, as one can see, his "vision" with simple dramaturgical effects giving the impression that he goes from darkness to light, that the passage is narrow and that he is under threat by hostile forces (the mullahs). The culminating "vision" is said to be momentary although he continues to describe it with extensive and detailed enthusiasm. This makes a striking contrast to the sarcasm he uses when seeing or mentioning sentimental versions of Islamic art; or when he condescendingly describes the giant Buddha-statues in Shibar, that became famous when blown up by the Taliban : "it is their negation of sense, the lack of any pride in their monstrous flaccid bulk, that sickens." (P. 315)

Byron: A young and arrogant Englishman with Eton manners and the imparted confidence of the Empire behind him. He is one in a long line of British travelers who are traveling to see, in the sense of acquiring, evaluating, conquering. He has Boswell and whisky in his luggage (yet also Proust and that sounds a little unusual for British 1930s). He is prompt in his critique of what he sees but his critical gaze is not only fixed on the foreign "Other" but on his "Own" to the same extent. He ironizes over himself and he satirizes the few Englishmen that come his way relentlessly. Here is how he imitates a distant Eton-acquaintance on a bar in Jerusalem trying to say that Sykes (Byron's fellow-traveler) should have a shave: "I mean to say, Sykes, you know, daffinitely, no I don't like to say, well I mean, daffinitely, never mind, I'd rather not say daffinitely /.../ I mean people might think you were a bit of a cad you know, daffinitely." (p. 25)

The most important indication of Byron as a modern travel writer is, however, that he permits himself to be overwhelmed by what he sees. His travelogue is only an effective frame to those visual revelations that he is looking for and always affected by. The conqueror allows himself to be conquered! As the example from the temple in Meshed shows, he must permit himself for a short while to *go native* in order to see what he wants to see. *Going native* is not only a practical maneuver, but also a theatrical and symbolic act: it means that you transform yourself into someone else in order to see this Otherness in its natural setting and condition. *Going native* is a strategy tempting several modern travelers to stray towards the perilous balance between the own and the other. More examples will be given when I come to Kapuściński and Seierstad; we will also meet quite contrasting strategies with travelers such as Naipaul and Canetti.

In the great Islamic art gallery, Byron is rushing around in order to see as much as possible but he is also capable of slowing down in order to be affected. He resists his own impulse to map and judge. He has a critical and evaluating gaze but he can also suspend his judgment and he can sometimes turn the critical gaze towards himself and his own British conditioning . He is certainly no impartial witness. I would sooner call him a critical, ironical and sometimes passionate witness.

*

Nicolas Bouvier left Geneva in June 1953 together with his friend, the artist Thierry Vernet, both heading for a long but unplanned journey. They had money for a couple of months, a tiny Fiat Topolino, a tape recorder, camera and notebooks. (If you want a glimpse of the journey there is a documentation of Bouvier as photographer in Bouvier's *Œuvres,* as published by Gallimard 2004, and at the art museum of Lausanne, homepage http://www.elysee.ch). The journey takes them to Macedonia, Anatolia, Iran, Pakistan and Afghanistan and when it ends one and a half years later, Bouvier sits alone at the Khyber Pass preparing to leave Afghanistan. Not for going home, however: this journey does not turn back but instead ends at the last moment. Bouvier's reader knows that he did not continue to Switzerland but went south, to India and Ceylon and spent a long period in Japan, as documented in *Chronique japonaise* (1975).

Bouvier is 24 years old when he leaves and it took 10 years before he finished the book about his great journey, *L'usage du monde* (1963) that has been translated as *The Way of the World* (1992) but the original title also conveys a sense of "using" the world or *savoir-vivre*. It is, in my opinion, one of the masterpieces of modern travel writing. Here, I restrict myself to some examples on the rhythm and visual strategy of the book and I shall start with the end. Bouvier has improvised his way through Asia with odd jobs and hardship and the book transforms this period into episodes and flashes. These are headed by a line informing us about place and perhaps name, rarely a date. The long journey does not consist of any epic or continual moving-on and Bouvier does not even include a map with his itinerary. The narration is instead about what happens when the traveler stops; it is more about the intermissions in the journey than about the journey itself. There are also a few italicized notes from the Now of the writing, "Six years later." The dating of the different episodes/glimpses do not indicate progress; instead the characteristics of the moment are hinted at: a season or a month or even time of the day: "Kandahar, three o'clock in the morning"; "A little later". You can read this text as a fragmentary diary, as repeated efforts of reconstruction. Perhaps as a collage where each individual piece comprises the intermissions of the journey but where the whole is nevertheless the journey itself.

The final episode is situated at the border of Afghanistan. We read that the narrator after one and a half years, at midday on December 5th, has reached the Khyber Pass. There, he stops, looks up and takes in the landscape:

> The mountain wouldn't waste itself in useless exertions: it rose from its powerful base, rested, and rose again, its flanks broad and its facets bevelled like jewels. On the lower peaks, the towers of Pathan strongholds shone as though rubbed with oil; the higher chamois-coloured slopes rose up behind them and broke off in shadowy circles into which drifting eagles disappeared in silence. And then slices of black rock where clouds snagged like wool. Towards the top, sixty-five thousand feet from my bank, there were narrow, gentle plateaux splashed with sunlight. The air was extraordinarily transparent. Voices carried. I could hear children shouting, far up on the old nomads' road, and the light footfall of invisible goats resounding down the whole pass with a crystalline echo. I spent a good hour without moving, drunk in this Apollonian landscape. Confronted by this prodigious anvil of earth and rock, the world of anecdote was like vanished. The mountain stretching out, the clear December air, the midday warmth, the sputter of the hookah, everything right down to the small change chinking in my pockets had become

elements of a plot in which I had arrived, after many obstacles, in time to play my part.[75]

Bouvier concludes this remarkable frozen moment by stating that it cannot last, that "nothing of that kind can be definitely acquired":

> Like water, the world ripples across you and endows its colors with you for a while. Then it recedes, and leaves you facing the void you carry inside yourself, confronting that central inadequacy of soul which you must learn to confront and to combat, and which, paradoxically, may be our prime mover. (ibid.)

I have quoted extensively to give an impression of the kind of *sight* that the traveler might expect slowing down and, as in this case, enduring so long that he approaches a state of meditation. The correct word for this sight, as in the case of Robert Byron, seems to be an *epiphany*: an illumination or a vision with dimensions of the sacred and sublime. With Bouvier as well as with Byron, it is, of course, a matter of secularized epiphanies. In Bouvier's case, it is transformed into philosophical meditation on the inconstancy of life and the necessity of morally handling the lack of meaning that inevitably replaces the moment that was experienced as saturated with meaning.

Bouvier, like Byron, permits himself to be overwhelmed in that he describes his young persona as overwhelmed. He goes even farther than Byron since he is not satisfied with a critical observation of what he sees. He also integrates his young persona into the landscape that makes up his view. As a small part: young Bouvier seeing the landscape is, of course, a minute part of what he sees but still a part that is as necessary as the woolly clouds and the shouting children, for instance.

Bouvier's narration is concluded in and by this moment — he only adds a few lines to indicate that it was now time for his young persona to cross the Pass and continue to the South. What makes young Bouvier sit down and take in the landscape — becoming a part of the landscape himself — is that he has reached the farthest end of his journey. He takes leave by resisting leaving. Bouvier's reader has long since noticed that elevated moments of this character, *sights* of epiphanic dimensions, have a tendency to turn up exactly when the narrator is about to cross a border, leaving one place for another. When he is preparing to leave Anatolia he stays awake through a clear night, waiting for a transport, again with mountains

---

75 P. 307. Transl. modified.

– Caucasus – in view: "Time passes in brewing tea, odd remarks, cigarettes, then dawn comes up, widens, quails and partridges are being heard … and you quickly anchor this superior moment like a dead body at the bottom of your memory, where you will look for it one day." (p. 90, transl. mod.)

The "superior moment" (*cet instant souverain*) is related to leaving here, to vigil and the light of dawn. Bouvier confirms that precisely such moments, which are even more "serene" than the moments of love, make up the "bedrock of existence" (*l'ossature de l'existence*). The most transient of everything – the moment – as the firm basis of existence!

The words used by Bouvier to characterize the moment, here translated to "serene" — *une lévitation plus sereine* — contribute to the quasi-sacred dimension that makes it possible to use a word like epiphany. The elevation (*lévitation*) returns in a context emphasizing the sacred as well as the visual. Bouvier is now in a mosque in Isphahan, Persia, where he first notices the "famously blue" color that he relates to Persian culture: "This time it is combined with a little turquoise, yellow and black which makes it vibrate and gives it that power of levitation [*lévitation*] which we usually associate with sanctity." (p. 191)

(I recommend a comparison with the extensive description of what I believe to be the same temple given by Robert Byron in *The Road to Oxiana*. Byron, as ever, stresses its architectural design but finishes – overwhelmed – by stating that it is "a richness of light and surface, of pattern and color only" that gives this mosque its unsurpassed "splendor". [p. 200] I would posit that Byron's *splendor* is not so far away from Bouvier's *lévitation*.)

Bouvier's "superior moments" (that are the time and place for his "sights") are charged with the approaching farewell but also with what has gone before. The moment is an interval in the continuity of the journey or a link between the different stations of the journey. Every component in Bouvier's grand collage consists of intervals and potential moments. These are arranged to link those "superior moments" that are in fact moments of rest: young Bouvier waiting for the dawn in the night of Anatolia or waiting for the crossing of the Khyber Pass. Bouvier is slowing down and "suspensing" his decisions in accordance with the recommendation given by Nietzsche when learning to see. There is nothing heroic in Bouvier's enterprise (as in Nietzsche's slogans), and nothing critical (as with Byron). Bouvier's gaze is *resting*. He permits his young self to stop and to linger in the situations that happen when he stops, in the *sights* to be seen, to bring to the surface, the memory that he once anchored and thus make his prose come to life.

*

Ryszard Kapuściński was a traveling journalist, a writer and a poet who was just as interested in literary borders as in political borders. Perhaps you could call this Polish reporter a man of the frontier since he had been traveling since the 1950s throughout Africa, Asia, South-America and the Soviet Union, always searching for borders, limits, extremes. In one example, from the book on the decaying Soviet Union, *Imperium* (1993): Kapuściński arranges a spectacular and risky adventure in order to visit the confined Armenians in Nagorno-Karabach. Why? "I wanted to be in this place at all cost, because I have always been moved by the fate of people condemned to extermination." (p. 242). He is, in other words, searching along the extremes of humanity in order to witness what no-one else has seen. And? Then he transforms himself into the literary medium of the seeing witness.

I am thinking now of *Imperium* and the Africa-book *The Shadow of the Sun* (*Heban* 1998). They are rather alike in terms of their construction: both consist of numerous comparatively short episodes and chapters that make up a visual, scenic and narrative unity. Like all travelogues, these books are retrospective. That does not stop Kapuściński (nor did it stop Robert Byron and Nicolas Bouvier) from using the present tense, direct speech, dialogue, *style indirect libre* to produce an impression of here and now: the view of the eyewitness. Both books form a kind of circle round their subject. In *Imperium*, Kapuściński travels around the Soviet Union although preferably along its outer borders, from the oriental Jerevan and Baku up to the arctic Vorkuta; in *The Shadow of the Sun* the voyage is from Ghana in the West to Ethiopia in the East. Both books are given a biographical frame. *Imperium* starts with a strong scene where the child Ryszard witnesses the deportation of his father and the book ends with Kapuściński returning 50 years later to his home-town where they still remember his parents. *The Shadow of the Sun* is subtitled "My African Life"; in both books it is a non-fictive Kapuściński speaking although the scenes are given a literary treatment. This does not mean that Kapuściński transforms himself into a literary figure with respect to, for instance, psychology, love affairs and development; rather he is the narrating voice and a character that exposes himself to extremes: experiencing, for instance, jungle-malaria, desert heat and Arctic cold. Both books mix a gaze of critical distance with solidarity and empathy. In *Imperium* the Soviet system is, of course, criticized, while its victims and in particular its ethnic minorities appeal for curiosity and empathy. "I am most fascinated by the mental and political decolonization of the world", he writes (p. 309). This fascination motivates his repeated visits to the Caucasian republics where more or less Oriental patterns take over when the Soviet power disintegrates.

Kapuściński heads for scenic demonstration, but he does not neglect critical analysis. He avoids a teaching position, even if he gives a "lecture" in *The Shadow of the Sun* (on Rwanda) and a thorough analysis (on the phenomenon Idi Amin). In *Imperium*, analytical quotations appear often. They are collected from historians and system-critics, but they are not presented as components of a comprehensive argument rather as voices making up a choir of testimonies. They contribute to making his text *polyphonic*, a word used by Kapuściński in the prelude to *Imperium*, with a kind of declaration:

> This book is written polyphonically, meaning that the characters, places, and themes that thread their way through its pages might reappear several times, in different years and contexts. However, in contrast to the principles of polyphony, the whole does not end with a higher and definitive synthesis, but, on the contrary, it disintegrates and falls apart, and the reason for this is that in the course of my writing the book, its main subject and theme fell apart – namely, the great Soviet superpower. (p. x)

In spite of this lack of a comprehensive whole, one can easily find thematic connections in both books. In *Imperium* the theme is related to borders: borderlines, border-crossings, border-disintegration. An early passage discusses our longing for the "limitless" and is followed by striking observations on the importance of the barbed wire for the Soviet State, the enormity and expanse of its production to satisfy the need for the barbed wire all along borders and around camps and barracks and weapon-depots. In *The Shadow of the Sun*, a play of light and darkness is thematized as well as African time being presented in different versions, as endurance and waiting: "Africa is eternal abiding".[76]

Cora Sandel situated her Alberta in the lingering-waiting position. Waiting comes close to the Rest, where Bouvier can at times recollect his young self. Compared to these slow wanderers, Kapuściński seems like a hectic traveler, permanently on his way along and across new borders. He does not travel, as Byron does, seeking visual sights (regardless of whether such sights do indeed arise, such as when the Siberian aurora borealis reveals the color Green to him). Kapuściński does not travel for a purpose or at least not for *one* purpose. Instead, he wants us to see a reality that is as plural as the "multilogical" Soviet reality. Therefore, he travels in all directions while rounding up his subjects – Africa, the Soviet empire. The result is not only "polyphonical" but also "polyvisual": Kapuściński transforms himself into a medium for the continent that he tries to listen to and witness in its full plurality. His gaze could be called *prismatic*: it gives us flashes and fragments of a whole, which is still not a homogeneous whole. Therefore, we must call Kapuściński a modernistic travel writer with poetical inclinations, breaking the linearity of time and travel in a prismatic plurality: in both books, progression is substituted by a plurality of moments. Straight interpretations become "multilogical" and compact reality is known only as fragments. Kapuściński transforms himself into a choir of testimonies and a cloud of witness.

*

Åsne Seierstad, like Kapuściński, heads for the frontier: she is best known for her admirable journalistic reports from war scenes in Kabul and Baghdad. I shall restrict myself here to the book in which she records the months she spent with an Afghan family after the fall of the Taliban : *The Bookseller of Kabul* (2002). The book was earlier mentioned in this chapter as an example of travel writing with documentary ambitions. I shall now discuss it as an interesting contribution to the problematic of visuality.

Seierstad subtitles the book "family drama"[77] and declares in a preface that she has chosen a "literary form" although she is describing "real events" (p. 3) — in interviews she has named her literary

---

76 Transl. Klara Glowczewska, Penguin 2002, p. 318
77 This has disappeared from the English edition.

form a "docu-novel". Authenticity is her agenda. This does not distinguish her from other travel writers, such as Kapuściński for instance. He is, as we have seen, a witness who wants us to believe his words and he uses literary technique to establish his credibility. Seierstad employs the strategy of many great predecessors: she tries to *go native*, dressing up in order to look like an Afghan woman, assuming the *burkha* when going out in the streets and sleeping on the floor with the women in the home of the bookseller.

What happens to the gaze of the visitor when he or she is trying to become a part of the foreign culture?

There is certainly no clear or simple answer to this: the examples I have already given display a great deal of variety. Sandel's Alberta becomes a fish in foreign water: she can see the Parisian reality from the inside but she can also run a critical eye over her Norwegian origin as well as the international Bohemia in Paris. Byron has a conquering and evaluating gaze but he also permits himself to be overwhelmed, to be seen. Kapuściński's prismatic gaze is a medium for the reality he sees, the gaze of a witness (or several witnesses).

Seierstad's gaze is also that of a witness, but of another kind still. Here is how she visualizes the matriarch of the family in the hammam: "The breasts hang down on each side. The belly, being so huge that it covers her sex when she sits or lies down, is spread out like a white, amorphic bulk."[78] When finished with the bath: "The women leave the baths and as they go one sees the dirt. Eggshells and rotten apples lurk in the corners. Lines of muck are left on the floors – the women use the same plastic sandals in the hammam as they do on the village paths, in the outside loos and in their backyards /…/ No one brought a change: they pull on the same clothes as the ones they arrived in." (p. 167f.)

"One" sees, the text says. "One" sees and witnesses what we readers could never see for ourselves. It is hard to believe that the Afghan gaze would be as disgusted as the "one" that sees here. It is rather a Western gaze using its anonymity to see on our behalf — but also to judge, to see what the Afghan women *should* see: the dirt.

Here is another Seierstad-example, it has to do with one of the boys in the family, Aimal, whom "became increasingly unwell and unhappy. His face turned pale and his skin sallow. His young body

---

[78] The passage has disappeared from the English edition and is translated by me from the Norwegian original (Cappelen 2002, p. 170).

stooped and lost its resilience." (P. 203) The reason being he has to tend to one of his father's shops all day long. "'The fatherless, poor Fazil can go to school', Aimal complained to Mansur, his older brother. 'But I, who have a father who has read all the books in the world, I have to work twelve hours a day. I should be playing football, have friends, run about', he complained."[79]

The narrator observes the body of the boy and listens to his complaint. Still we have to suspect that she manipulates the testimony by putting words in the boy's mouth. (Has she really listened to this conversation? In which language has it been related? Has she invented it as a literary way of making a documentary impression?) The use of direct speech indicates authenticity, still we wonder if the Afghan boy actually wants to play football all day and if he really can reflect on his situation in those words. The emerging problem of credibility is well known from ethnographic research, as well as from many versions of travel writing. The problem can be described as a suspicion that the narrator *colonizes* the Afghan reality that she describes.

Let me try to clarify: I have of course no reason to believe that Åsne Seierstad would have colonial inclinations. Furthermore, I fully agree with her set of values when it comes to hygiene and child education, not to mention that which is most prominent in her agenda and motivates the majority of her judgments: women's right to self-determination. When I find her writing problematic nevertheless, there are *aesthetical* reasons for this (and aesthetics in this case verges on ethics). The problem can be located to the "docu-novel" that she has chosen to write: it has grown out of the "new journalism" and the "documentary novel" of the sixties. These strategies are now affiliated with the kind of aesthetics developed in visual media: news programs with quasi-documentary elements, documentaries with hidden cameras, "docu-soaps" and so forth. The problematic involved has no simple solutions: travel writing is not a "genre" with pre existing rules and every travel writer has to make up their own contract to regulate the use of literary technique. As we have seen, Seierstad's contract — the "docu-novel" — includes the strategy of *going native*, which so many travel writers have previously successfully employed. When Seierstad transforms herself into a kind of *spy* with the mission of literally *unveiling* Afghan culture, she runs the risk of presenting it as an *inversion* of her own. The mechanism

---

79 Ibid. Transl. modified.

comes close to the one described by the philologist François Hartog, as quoted earlier when describing the workings of Herodot: "there is no longer an *a* and a *b*, but simply an *a* and the inversion of *a*." When compared with the examples from Seierstad: the hammam is dirty (inversion of the norm); the women do not change clothes after the bath (do.); the matriarch is fat (do.); the boy works behind a counter (inversion of the norm: to go to school, to "run about"). The inverted gaze is evaluating and judging even though the norms involved are never made explicit.

Perhaps the hidden camera would be the best characteristic for Seierstad's strategy. When she transforms herself to the "one" that "sees", she can witness what would not otherwise be seen. Her gaze is steadily watching Afghan reality. In order to unveil *them*, she must veil herself: she must conceal her gaze (that is to say her perspective), including the norms that are part of it and her focus and judgment according to this perspective. "I was there" is transformed into "we are there".

*

V. S. Naipaul is a writer motivated by the journey. There is a travelogue in practically everything that he has written. It seems as if he cannot travel without including his journey in a literary project and he does not seem to be able to develop literary projects without traveling. One could say perhaps that he explores new contracts for the literary coexistence between novel, autobiography, journalistic report and travelogue — and with the journey as a common denominator. Clearly, it is tempting to relate this traveling project so to speak with Naipaul belonging to several cultures in conjunction with his lack of belonging to any *one* culture: he is English when it comes to language and mature culture but he has a family background in Trinidad and an Indian background behind this. In *The Enigma of Arrival* (1987) he adopts an observing position regarding English culture and English landscape, as though he were a foreign visitor on an occasional visit. When the book changes perspective with a journey back to Trinidad, we realize that he takes on the observing perspective of the foreigner even there. When Naipaul travels in India (he has written three substantial travel books from India during different epochs of his life), he insists on his European perspective; in England he shifts to an Indian or Caribbean stance. I would like to say a little more about this shifting of perspectives, this *shifting gaze*, with the assistance of *The Enigma of Arrival*.

Naipaul calls the book a "novel", a term that invites qualification: the book is actually an autobiographical meditation and travelogue included. The main part consists of the narrator's observations along with reflections formed in his cottage in South England. There he works and there he observes life on the manor and its surroundings. It is a rural setting with both archaic and modern components: we are close to Stonehenge but also close to a military Air force base. The narrator observes what seems to be the invariability of life in this idyll; he is a viewer from the outside, observing incomprehensible but also unshakeable rituals. Nevertheless, dramatic changes occur with the passing of time, due to new conditions of production, due to the human frailty, but also due to time itself in the guise of illness and death. The narrator observes these changes also until he is stricken by illness and prepares to leave his cottage.

Naipaul interrupts this effort to render the English country-life as at once archaic-invariable and permanently changing, with a biographical memory: his first journey from Trinidad to New York and hence from New York via boat to England, his arrival in London and his early efforts to become a writer. He closes the book with a short episode from Trinidad: by now his sister has died and he returns to take part in the Hindu funeral rituals. We understand that it is only after this trip that he is fully prepared to write about his life in England.

The book thereby commutes between arrival and homecoming on an axis of origin and destination. This traffic is coordinated with shifts between permanence and change, observed by the narrator from his cottage. The gazing narrator is simultaneously naïve and reflected and his perspective is due to an intricate combination of intimacy and distance. The narrator has become just as native as the natives themselves and therefore possesses a privileged perspective of observing what happens so to speak from the inside. This is not *going native* as a strategy for assimilation. Indeed Naipaul demonstrates the *impossibility* of finding a stable perspective and an authentically belonging in a world, which is characterized by permanent change. Naipaul – not unlike Alberta in Paris – has multiple belongings, which makes him at home everywhere at the same time as being a stranger everywhere. It is only when he steps back to either recall or visit his origin that he can place himself at a sufficient distance to make it possible for him to describe English reality from the inside out. That does not mean that the origin offers an authentic identity: the origin has become just as foreign as the destination. It is the *shifting* between origin and destination that is the basis for Naipaul's observations. That makes traveling vital to his writing, as an activity and as a motor — and I would think that it is this very mechanism that has made him the target of some "post-colonial" criticism.

Naipaul's version of sightseeing is a gaze that shifts between intimacy and distance. Owing to this shifting, he is capable of seeing reality from the inside as well as from the outside. In Naipaul's world this means seeing reality as it is, as his world and reality are just as shifting as his gaze: in *The Enigma of Arrival* he is trying to fixate on a seemingly invariable existence as *a world in flux*.[80] Naipaul's overarching project seems to be to teach himself (and us) to learn to live with this law: to endure. "Flux" is not regarded as decay but as necessary *change*: "I lived not with the idea of decay /.../ so much as with the idea of change. I lived with the idea of change, of flux, and learned, profoundly, not to grieve for it." (P. 190)

*

I conclude this review with a provocative and enigmatic example.

Elias Canetti spent some time in Marrakesh in the 1950s. He was a tourist, walking around, using his eyes for very literal sight seeing. Later, he wrote the "notes after a journey" that were published as *The Voices of Marrakesh* (as mentioned earlier on in this chapter). The book consists of a series of short, novelistic texts made up of voices and visual impressions: sketches in prose that are variations on the meeting between the narrator and Moroccan reality. I wish to discuss these sketches as a final version of visual strategy. While Canetti is indeed a traveler using his eyes (he slows down and tries to learn to see), his seeing, however, is met with unexpected frustrations.

Canetti wants to see camels. The first one he sees has rabies, when he finally spots a camel-caravan outside the town-walls, he learns that the camel-drivers are not heading for any picturesque desert-adventures at all but have a more mundane destination: the slaughterhouse. When he watches a a holy man, a "marabou," putting coins he is given into his mouth, he is astonished and cannot help staring — until he realizes that he is the one that the crowd regards

---

80 Penguin 1987, p. 53.

as a curiosity. In the Jewish Mellah-quarters, he feels at home — "I found exhibited the same density and warmth of life as I feel in myself. I *was* the square as I stood in it. I believe I am it always" (p. 45) — until he is pursued by beggars into the most ill advised regions of the quarters and comes to suspect that the cozy Mellah conceals another, invisible town. At the marketplace, Djema-el-Fna, Canetti is excited when he hears the oral narrators — he makes a point of not learning one word of Arabic because he naïvely wants to imagine the narrators as "an enclave of ancient, untouched existence." (p. 78) He ponders on the decay that was caused by writing but soon discovers that the professional scribes sit only a few feet from the oral narrators at the same market. Outside his favorite restaurant, he imagines striking up a rapport of sorts with a little girl who persists in making amusing gestures; that is until the owner informs him that the gestures are invitations and that the girl is available for sale at 50 francs. At the night bar he watches a handsome young couple and attempts to fancy their doings in life; he later learns that the husband has homosexual relationships with members of the nobility and forces his wife into prostitution.

The list goes on. Nothing is what it seems to be for Canetti's gaze. The *sights* he sees do not conform to his expectations. His tourist gaze is met with resistance: the foreign reality stays foreign. Moreover, the tension between his own expectations and the other culture is played out as a threatening difference and opacity. When Canetti in his subtitle stresses that his sketches are written *after* the journey it seems to mean that he does not want to permit memory and afterthought to be reconciliatory. All travelogues are written after the fact but most travel writers try to hide this by endowing their narratives with a touch of presence. Canetti also presents his sketches as authentic and gives the impression of being on the spot; while still emphasizing distance. He enters what Mary Louise Pratt called a *contact zone* (as was quoted earlier). Although Pratt had classical examples in mind, her term can also be applied to the modern project: the meeting between the "own" and the "foreign". Canetti enters his *contact zone* in order to make way for a meeting that is *neither* reconciliatory *nor* assimilating. Instead, Canetti's meetings are frustrating and alienating. This obviously distinguishes them not only from Pratt's classical examples but also from productive and overwhelming meetings of the kind we have seen through my earlier examples. Canetti's version of meeting and seeing comes to nothing.

This is indeed an unusual situation in travel writing. The tensions of the meeting between the own and the foreign have been presented in terms of gaze: Sandel's gaze is cubist, Byron's is conquering yet overwhelmed, Bouvier's is meditative, Naipaul's is shifting, Kapuściński's is prismatic, Seierstad's is colonizing— they all enact a kind of interaction between the traveler and the foreign reality. Canetti does not make even the slightest effort to *go native* or to adjust his gaze and he exposes his own expectations and prejudice. But he stays in his *contact zone* long enough for the foreign culture to demonstrate its foreign nature. He does not remain there in order to understand; instead he remains in order to fully realize that he and we cannot understand.

An expressive allegory for this predicament is given in the last sketch of the book, "The Unseen" [*Der Unsichtbare*], meaning the one that cannot be seen or the invisible. Canetti is once more at the marketplace, where he has discovered "a small, brown bundle on the ground" (p. 100f.), *ein Bündel* [a bundle] that has no voice yet nevertheless emits a simple sound, a lengthy *e-e-e-e*. The narrator examines this "bundle" every night and is fascinated by the sound: he can see no mouth, not even a face under the brown hood, so where does the sound come from? What does it mean? Perhaps, the narrator speculates, it (the bundle) has no tongue making it impossible to pronounce the consonant in "Allah" and compelling it to restrict itself to the vowel sounds. How does the bundle reach the crowded market and how does it make its living? Canetti registers two feelings when looking at the bundle: impotence — due to his incapability in penetrating the mystery of the bundle — and a benevolent pride [*Stolz*] — for its very life.

Impotence on his own behalf, pride on behalf of the other. Sightseeing, according to Canetti's version, is therefore a matter of *not* being able to see but of realizing that what you cannot see exists nevertheless and has a value of some kind. The lesson of seeing seems to be a lesson of restriction: learning the limits from what you can see. Of course, such a lesson results in impotence, but also what Canetti refers to as *Stolz*. The sightseer experiences pride because this incomprehensible foreign life is just that, life.

There is a degree of ambivalence in all of my examples. Such is the nature of travel writing: it hovers between fact and fiction, between oneself and the foreign other, between mapping and seeing. Canetti's ambivalence seems different. He is not a witness (we cannot rely on him). He is not mapping: he displays no "anxiety to map the globe" or reinstall "ethnocentrically superior attitudes." He may be entering what Mary Louise Pratt called a "contact zone" but his efforts do not yield any contact. His sightseeing ends in blindness and he invites the suspicion that the project of modern travel writing is ultimately doomed to failure. Canetti is perhaps giving us a nihilistic version of travel writing. Alternatively, he is reminding us of the difficulties and risks involved whenever we try to understand and meet the foreign other. Needless to say, I wish to regard this intriguing episode as an allegorical version of *prose*: as prosaic reality along with the frustrating physics of literary prose as well as a glimpse of the frustrated metaphysics of prose.

Exiles: life writing

In this chapter I shall present a review of modern and modernist writers who are aiming at constructing or reconstructing themselves in their writing. I call this *life writing* and the writers under discussion are Anaïs Nin, Witold Gombrowicz, Anna Banti, Czesław Miłosz, Vladimir Nabokov, Elias Canetti, Michael Ondaatje, Thomas Bernhard and Orhan Pamuk. It goes without saying that these prominent writers all provide different versions of the task of writing their selves. Nevertheless, they all have at least two characteristics in common: the life-writing ambition, combined with a predicament that can be summarized in one word – exile. While each of them has their own solution to the literary task, it is the underlying motivation – exile – that makes them exemplary. Exile is the short name for the psycho-social scenario that seems to characterize the 20th century and even extends to other eras. Oswald Spengler, in *Der Untergang des Abendlandes* (1918–22), already stigmatized the intellectuals of his time as being *nomadic*; thereby preparing for the ruin of a civilization built on deep-rooted and stable affiliations. Needless to say, I value the modern versions of Diaspora differently and do not regard my writers as simple symptoms of a situation that surpasses the individual (albeit one which then influences all individuals). I prefer to think that my writers *show the way*; or that they show different ways for prose on the frontline of modern prose: often beyond fiction, always working with the modern experience summarized as exile.

The classical motivation for autobiographical life writing was simply death: approaching death provided the incentive to sum up and attempt to install some meaning into the chaos of a life lived. Foreboding versions of death could either be departures or other forms of breaking up, installing abrupt changes and motivating retrospective reflection. In modern times, the breaking up was frequently a definite and coerced change of life conditions. Exile, or a lighter version thereof, was perhaps also a latent motivation for classical life writers, such as Montaigne and Rousseau, although it has become yet more important for the moderns. Something has arisen that definitively separates the pioneers from the moderns; this new element is *loss*. If death motivated the classical writing of the self, then exile and loss are decisive for the moderns. Now the self is no longer a mysterious, unknown continent to be discovered. Rather, the self is a lost or sunken continent to be rediscovered. The most important capacity in the writing of the self is: Memory. Loss triggers those memorial and life writing strategies that I shall present here as *showing, searching* and *concealing* – all of which contributes to the *reconstruction* of the self. The writing of the self has always had an element of construction. In modern times, self-fashioning, foregrounding and profiling accentuate the fact that self-writing is concerned with the constructive creation of a self; or a reconstruction – now that an original identity has been lost.

I shall start with two examples of literary diary: these are exceptions to the observations that I have just summarized, in the sense that death and memory are of little significance here. Diaries try to come close to lived experience and death signalizes the end rather than the beginning for the diary-writer. Diary writing, on the other hand, emphasizes the construction and the self-fashioning aspects involved in the writing of the self. This is my impression of, for instance, Kafka who wrote an exemplary literary diary, exemplary in the sense that his diary writing was closely related to his literary writing. Self-fashioning also characterizes the two examples I shall use here: Anaïs Nin and Witold Gombrowicz. They offer strategies for foregrounding, fashioning and constructing their selves – they show themselves in writing.

*

Anaïs Nin wrote a diary from her 11th year and with varying intensity for the rest of her life. Altogether she is said to have produced 35,000 handwritten pages carefully kept in what she called "iron-boxes", pages that she translated (from Spanish and French into English) and, late in life, also published (as excerpts). The diary took up a great deal of her time and was apparently an important part of her life. She claims to have started writing it as a letter to her father who left the family only to reappear by the time of the first published volume, loved and hated. We are given the impression that he, like all men in her vicinity, has amorous feelings for her. The importance of the diary is further stressed in the diary itself. The writing of the diary is constantly commented upon and she regularly shows parts of it to interested men, with the unfailing result that their interest increases.

The first published volume from 1966 goes back to 1931, when she is approaching 30 years of age and living a turbulent life in Paris. According to the editor, the volume gives us about half of the real diary; in other words, Nin has cut and spliced a presentable volume. This documents her meetings with Henry Miller, who lived what he later called "quiet days in Clichy"; also his wife June, presented as extravagant and fatal; and also different psychoanalysts culminating in Otto Rank, who tries to make Nin less dependent on her diary. Nin paints a devoted portrait of Rank, ranging from conversations to small essays. The treatment has a bizarre consequence in that for a while the diary reports her efforts to stop writing a diary: "The period without the diary remains an ordeal. Every evening I wanted my diary as one wants opium."[81] Finally, she returns to normal writing. Instead of her falling under the influence of Dr. Rank we are given the impression that he is falling for her. As is the typical outcome when men meet with Nin and her diary. The published version cultivates an erotic atmosphere but stays away from sex.

The diary displays a rich literary repertoire: it gives us scenes and essayist philosophical reflection with a feminist profile, it poses questions, quotes letters, relates meetings and paints portraits. The culmination is the strong scene where Nin miscarries prematurely and the child is stillborn. Nin wants to document that she was not fit for normal family life, with the implication that she had to devote her life to literature. Literature is indeed a prominent theme: she keeps reminding herself and her readers that she is heading for literature. She wants the diary as well as her explicitly literary writing to be read by her friends. She also uses the diary to maintain a distance from everyday nuisances: "This is what I do with the diary, carries it along everywhere, writes on coffee-tables while waiting for a friend, in the waiting-rooms, while my hair is being washed, in Sorbonne when the lecture becomes dull, when I travel, on excursion, almost when people are talking to me." (*Journals*, p.155) The diary becomes

---

81   *The Journals of Anaïs Nin, 1931–1934*, London: Harvest 1966, p. 307. Will be quoted with pages in the text.

the indispensable tool for handling life and for making life literary: "My diary is my book of work. Everything I can use in novels is put in the diary." (*Journals*, p. 58)

The literary character is accentuated by Nin's habit of giving novelistic titles to the notebooks she used for her diary-writing. This effect has disappeared from the 1960s' editions as well as from the so-called "unexpurgated" editions published posthumously. In the 1960s, the diary has the character of a literary workshop, where Nin is testing different styles, forms and interpretations in order to construct her life as literature. The edition from 1986 (*Henry and June*) has been collated from six notebooks and the edition from 1992 (*Incest*) from more than twenty. In both cases the diary becomes a journal reporting on a hectic life; literary ambitions have not disappeared but they have been pushed to the background. While these versions may be "unexpurgated", they still comprise a selection, excluding most of what we read in the editions from the 1960s.

The 1986 version, *Henry and June*, tells us about the important role played by Henry Miller during this period (1931–32). The 1992 version, *Incest*, covers up until the culminating birth of the previous version — which now appears to be a late abortion. The prominent presence of the husband Hugo is a radical change, as he was suspiciously absent from the 1966 version. The earlier version concerns writing and feminist reflection in an erotic atmosphere; now it is sex. We are given a rich portrait of the turbulent sex-life with Henry. The husband also receives his fair share of exposure, although these reports are less enthusiastic. In *Incest* we also meet with the father, who has an intense adventure with his daughter, plus her different analysts culminating with Otto Rank. We follow Anaïs from bed to bed, meaning that she writes of her copulation with number one while going to bed with number two and consults her psychoanalyst while she on her way to number three. In this version, Nin is less reflecting; instead she registers in the present tense, giving the impression that she is writing (and we are reading) in the very Now of the event itself. Here is Henry Miller, together with his buddy Fred visiting Anaïs:

> Their admiration and love is sweet to me. I lose my sense of secrecy. I open the iron boxes and show them my early journals. Fred grasps the first volume and begins to cry and laugh over it. I have given Henry the

red journal, all about himself, a thing I have never done with anyone. I read over his shoulder.[82]

Maybe she is writing behind his back? This massive manifestation of immediacy contributes to the impression that we are following Anaïs' shifting activities and moods as they are shifting. This concentration on men and sex and also on immediacy, contributes to making the later versions more conservative in terms of the aesthetics and morality of life writing. The "unexpurgated" Anaïs we meet is a victim of temporary physical and sentimental whims. In the earlier version she is reflecting and working and aiming for literature. This impression is due to the selections of the later versions and their aesthetics of immediacy. Anaïs Nin herself aimed for more than that. This is evident from the fact that even the later versions include more than sex. Nin is quoting herself from long letters and other works, showing that the diary, even in this form, is a literary workshop. Nin realizes that the men she is meeting are given a literary profile when they enter her diary. Even Henry Miller is given an imaginary touch: "I created Henry as I needed him. I also *invented* Henry!"[83] A remarkable instance of the diary as a mediator between life and literature occurs when her husband Hugo suddenly discovers some of her infidelities as a result of her forgetting to lock up her latest notebook. She replies that what he has read is only phantasm, the real diary is still to be read:

> And when I saw his face I began to lie, to lie eloquently. "You only read the invented journal. It is all invention, to compensate for all I don't do — believe me, I'm a monster, but only imaginatively. You can read the *real* journal anytime. Ask Allendy [her therapist]. He knows about the invented journal. He called me '*la petite fille littéraire*'. (Incest, p. 268)

Anaïs starts living up to the description of being a literary girl by producing an imaginary and non-erotic diary offered to her husband as the real one. The "unexpurgated" diary that *we* read is on the other hand presented as the real thing. We never doubt the truth of her diary: that she lived a turbulent life with many men. Still, the relentless use of immediacy and present tense contributes to making the real thing into a literary thing. This life, not least in its erotic dimension, is interwoven with literature. The diaries of Anaïs Nin make up a literary project: she is constructing herself by showing.

---

82 *Henry and June*. Penguin 1990 (1986), p. 123.
83 *Incest*. London: Harvest 1992, p. 220. Will be quoted with pages in the text.

*

Witold Gombrowicz, the Polish writer, also has a famous diary, the majority of which was published during his lifetime. He is not *showing* himself to the same extent as Nin; indeed he is even secretive about his private life, but he certainly adds a new dimension when it comes to the task of *constructing* the self. Gombrowicz started writing his diary in the beginning of the 1950s, when he had already been exiled in the Argentine for many years. He lived in a distant culture and with a language that remained foreign to him — compared to Anaïs Nin for instance, who seemed to effortlessly switch between languages and cultures. Perhaps Gombrowicz regarded this situation as a task rather than as a problem? In 1953, he comments in his diary upon something written by another famous exile writer, the Romanian E. M. Cioran, on "Advantages and disadvantages of exile." Gombrowicz concentrates on the "immense stimulus" of emigration:

> For lo and behold the country's elite is kicked out of the border. It can think, feel, and write from the outside. It gains distance. It gains an incredible spiritual freedom. All bonds burst. One can be more oneself. In the general din all the forms that have existed until now loosen up and one can move toward the future in a more ruthless way.[84]

Gombrowicz puts this in italics because he is quoting himself from an article on the subject. His diary was public from the beginning as it was published in the exile-journal *Kultura*, giving him the opportunity to quote chosen parts from his essayist and journalistic writing.

He does not quote his more literary work even though he discusses it extensively. He frequently uses his diary while investigating the numerous horrible misunderstandings that he was exposed to by other literary exiles in the Polish Diaspora. In contrast to Kafka, he rarely uses his diary as a workshop, which includes literary sketches. In contrast to Nin, he rarely gives us scenes from actual life as raw material for literary processing. We get the impression that he regards the diary as a fundamentally different discourse from his literary efforts. This impression is confirmed by a reading of his novelistic *Transatlantik* (1953). Here he deals with some of those

---

84 I quote from Lillian Vallee's translation of the diaries in two volumes, Northwestern University Press, 1988. Reference will be given in the text, here I: 40.

experiences that we also glimpse in the diary, but differently: here they are bizarre, comical, "literary".

The main purpose of his diary is the foregrounding of his own existence and exploiting being uprooted and the freedom of the émigré in order to construct himself as a figure of literary relevance. There are many comments on contemporary philosophy from Sartre to Foucault, many powerful judgments on Polish literature, many investigations of his own writing. Above all, there is a self-fashioning subject profiling himself and relating himself to those qualities that he regards as the most important qualities in literature: youthfulness, style, form. "I can defend myself against this" he writes — defend against being misunderstood, underestimated, made invisible — "only by defining myself, only by delineating myself endlessly." (I: 92) The diary is the ideal form for this task since it permits Gombrowicz to comment upon anything and anyone while continually describing himself. Every notice contributes to the construction of "myself" in what he considers as his project: "To commence creating myself and to make a character like Hamlet or Don Quijote out of Gombrowicz – ? – !" (I: 113)

The result would be tiresome to read should Gombrowicz not write mostly indirectly about himself while writing directly about others. Likewise should he not realize that his self is not a solipsistic entity but related to others and dependent on others. He asks himself "Who am I?" — a question that has been asked in life writing tradition at least since Montaigne. Gombrowicz focusses the question on the "am" rather than the "I": he gives the "I" a sociological determination and opens the way for regarding it as a construction, as a provisional arrangement. "Who am I? 'Am' I at all? From time to time 'I' am this or that." (I: 193) His insistent self-promotion can be regarded as role-playing, his self as a potentiality, as a result rather than a given point of departure. The self in itself is nothing at all or it is a mission to be accomplished. He arrives at the conclusion that the consciousness of oneself does not come *out* of us: "Doesn't awareness – that forced extreme awareness – arise among us, not from us, as something created by effort etc." (I: 181) The Gombrowicz self is neither natural, metaphysical nor a sociological entity; rather it is a discursive location. The writing of a diary means situating yourself in a position that permits you to go beyond conventional roles and define yourself. By making the self dependent on discourse, Gombrowicz excludes not only the romantic authorial self but all possible views of the self as given by nature, including gender-positions. Like an early constructivist, Gombrowicz insists on creating "a different position for myself – beyond man and woman – which would nevertheless not have anything to do with a 'third sex' – an asexual and purely human position from which I could begin airing these stuffy and sexually flawed areas." (I: 145) It is this relativized view of the self — the self as a discursive potentiality — that Gombrowicz is promoting and constructing in his diary, not least in his self-promotion. Even when he exclaims "I am" in order to confirm that his mission with the diary is accomplished: "This awareness: that I have already become myself. I already am. Witold Gombrowicz, these two words, which I carried on myself, are now accomplished. I am." (I: 172)

Gombrowicz uses his diary to concentrate some ideas of the self that were budding within literature, philosophy and sociology in his day: "In me, certain ideas that are in the air we all breathe are joined in a special and uniquely Gombrowiczian sense and I am this sense." (I: 94). Of course, he is not oblivious to the fact that such egocentric writing of himself can be read as, exactly that, egocentric. He comments upon this with characteristic distance by suddenly writing about himself in the third person:

> *Confessing to all of the pettiness of his greatness with a completely unheard-of insolence, boring, tormenting, irritating with his growing, he could change his confession into a first-class literary scandal, and himself into a freakish clown of greatness.* (II: 123)

It is just as characteristic that he then concludes this effort to write a piece of diary in the third person by proclaiming this a radical innovation: "*And this was something new, which he had never encountered in any of the diaries he had read — just imagine how enriching: to be able to talk about oneself in the first as well as the third person!*" (II: 128)

Talking about oneself in the first as well as the third person is merely the grammatical consequence of the double perspective that is presupposed in all forms of the literary writing of the self. The self being written about is always somewhere else and at sometime other than the self that is writing. There is always a self being written about by the writing self and the relation between the two varies: from distant to intimate. Montaigne has already used this distinction, in the famous passage quoted in my first chapter. Montaigne states that his book has created himself just as much as he has created the book, "a book of one substance with its author, proper to me and a limb of my life."[85] Gombrowicz offers his own version: "To a certain degree my books are a result of my life – but my life was formed in a greater measure from them and with them." (II: 11)

The classical tradition of the literary writing of the self is developed by modern literary diaries (as exemplified by Nin and Gombrowicz) into constructing a literary self that is relativized, decentered, critical, egocentric, whimsical, nihilistic. Gombrowicz, who died in 1969, probably has the last word in this modernist development of the self, already verging on the postmodern. It is difficult to imagine comparable literary diaries today. On the other hand we are faced with new medium in the internet, one that permits practically anyone to construct a web log (blog), thereby continually presenting and developing novel and diary-like versions of the literary self. I will touch upon this phenomenon in my last chapter. Here, I shall continue my review of modern and modernistic life writing strategies with some novelistic and autobiographical examples.

*

Anna Banti, the penname for Lucia Lopresti, Italian art-critic, historian and novelist, published the novel *Artemisia* in 1947. It is a biographical novel narrating the life of the 17th century painter Artemisia Gentileschi. My reason for presenting it here is its interesting autobiographical dimension. Banti started writing the novel during the war but a major part of the manuscript subsequently disappeared and she had to start anew. Maybe it was this unfortunate situation that provoked her to mingle biography with autobiography, making both into life writing. Perhaps it helped that the biographical information about the painter is scarce: there are some paintings, now famous, but few biographical facts, which may invite biographical construction and speculation. The result is a fascinating version of life writing as filtered through historic and biographical imagination; an intricate exchange between searching, showing and concealing.

There is nothing remarkable in writing about yourself by writing about others. It may even serve as a rule for the biographical project: to allow your own biography to influence your writing about others. Why confine this to the biographical project; why not also the monographic, historic, critical, philosophical…? (Maybe

---

85   *Essays*, transl. M. A. Screech, Penguin Classics 1991, p. 755.

my own quasi-exiled situation influences my writing this chapter.) Banti radicalizes this interaction between subject and object — or this interference — by making her own writing-situation a significant part of her story. Above all, she creates a dialogue with the historic material: Anna starts talking with Artemisia. This means that Artemisia stands out as a projection of Anna, but also that Anna herself results from the work with Artemisia. In other words, it means that the construction is problematized at the same time as being profiled: the construction of the biographical figure, of history, the construction of the self.

The novel starts with the narrator crying at the remains of her ruined home: "Under the rubble of my house I have lost Artemisia, my companion from three centuries ago who lay breathing gently on the hundred pages I had written."[86] The rest of the book is an effort to reconstruct what has been lost. Constructing the biography means handling the loss that is the starting point for the writing of the biography as well as the writing of the self. Early on, "I" becomes "she" – Artemisia. Then Artemisia becomes the "I" of her own narrative in dialogue with her narrator. After Artemisia has related her account of the rape she has been subjected to, the narrator comments: "Now it is for my benefit alone that Artemisia recites her lesson; she wants to prove to me that she believes everything that I invented." (*Artemisia*, p. 17) Still, Artemisia gets the upper hand in the sense that the story of her life grows. Even if it can only become a fragmentary and speculative biography, Banti gives us a fascinating portrait. I am tempted to say that the portrait of Artemisia is comparable to (and in dialogue with) the portraits executed by Artemisia herself, which exist to this day.

Within and behind this portrait, we recognize the narrator, whom calls attention to herself, starts a dialogue. Of course, that was not a foreign concept in the portraits of the Baroque period when surprising changes of perspective were commonplace (the most famous example is probably Velasquez' *Las Meninas*). A contract is established between the narrating biographer and Artemisia. The narrator complains: "I will never be able to be free of Artemisia again; she is a creditor, a stubborn, scrupulous conscience to which I grow accustomed as to sleeping on the ground. It is no longer our conversations

---

86 *Artemisia*, transl. Shirley D'Ardia Caracciolo, London: Serpent's Tail 1995 (1988), p. 4. References will be given in the text.

that bind me, as in the early days, but a sort of contract legally drawn up between lawyer and client, and which I must honor." (*Artemisia*, p. 33) Alternatively, the relationship can be referred to as a "chasing game" (*Artemisia*, p. 95), consisting of hide and seek and pursuit. Another possibility is that the relationship can grow cold: Artemisia disappears for the narrator, who must go looking for her to provoke her reactions.

The biography investigates the little that we know about the historic Artemisia: she was subjected to early sexual abuse but managed, against all odds, to take the perpetrator to court. She was permanently seeking her father, who was always distant. The father was also a famous artist whom ended up as a court painter in London, to where Artemisia travels in a final bid to establish contact. She develops her artistry, stubbornly and not without success, but at the expense of her marriage and her children. This is mirrored in our notions of the narrator: Anna Banti's writing of herself. Nothing is said about her father, husband, children or career, nor are we told about any sexual violence — only indirectly, through her manner of portraying Artemisia. What we do learn is that the politically and morally exposed position in the ruins of war is the starting point for the narrator and that she has suffered a decisive loss. She has lost her manuscript and maybe that is symbolic of all that was lost during the war: the lost manuscript is Banti's version of modern exile. We also learn that the narrator travels to England, both before and after the war, in the search for Artemisia and her father. In England, she finds what may indeed be a self-portrait of Artemisia only to lose sight of it again. Banti reflects: "Whether it is a self-portrait or not, a woman who paints in sixteen hundred and forty is very courageous, and this counts for ... at least a hundred others, right up to the present. 'It counts for you too,' she concludes by the light of a candle, in this room rendered gloomy by war, a short, sharp sound. A book has been closed, suddenly." (*Artemisia*, p.199)

It is hardly possible to decide if this last line – *It counts for you too* — is related to the narrator or to Artemisia, such is the intensity of their dialogue. I am certain, however, that the book, "whether it is a self-portrait or not," is written by a "very courageous" woman. Banti dares to defy literary conventions and most probably other conventions at the same time, when writing herself in and through Artemisia.

*

Banti's driving force for her version of life writing was loss. For the Polish poet and essayist *Czesław Miłosz* it was exile. This theme is found in all his writings although here I shall concentrate on his autobiographical book, *Rodzinna Europa* from 1958; the English translation was published as *Native Realm: a Search for Self-definition* in 1968. The original title (if not the translation) already reveals that Miłosz is not aiming at "defining" himself in any private or sentimental manner. Instead, he profiles himself as representative. It is about the self in Europe and also as a part and version of Europe. Put more exactly, it is a book about the "Eastern European" that was sadly unknown and unappreciated by Western Europeans. At the time of writing, the European Union was inaugurated in Western Europe; since which Westerners have had a tendency to view themselves as the sole authentic Europe. Miłosz wants, in other words, to present himself as part of an historic and political process. This is unusual amongst the moderns discussed here: they may well relate to history but rarely as a part of it; instead as concealed in history or as in contrast or conflict to history. With the previously touched upon Gombrowicz and Banti, the war is a presupposition and a background but never a theme. Only with Orhan Pamuk, to whom we shall return, do we find a writer who inscribes himself into topical political processes. In my gallery of modern authors, it is Miłosz alone whom consequently reads a general history in his own history and makes the war experience central to his life experience.

East European history coincides with Miłosz' life history: he was born 1911 in Vilnius, then in Poland and part of a heterogeneous and conflict-ridden region. The town did not even have a solid name: "Poles say Wilno; Lithuanians Vilnius; Germans and Belarusians, Wilna."[87] During Miłosz' time, the town and its region has wandered from Poland to Lithuania to Germany to the Soviet Union. It has been composed of several ethnic groups; furthermore it has been divided between Catholics and Jews. According to Miłosz, most of them had one "fatherland" in common: the Polish language. (*Native Realm*, p. 102) Moreover, the region inevitably was a victim of the many forms of destruction and migration that have defined the modern history of Eastern Europe.

---

87   *Native Realm*, transl. Catherine S. Leach, Penguin 1988, p. 55. Reference will be given in the text.

Miłosz concludes his memories from the heterogeneous character of his early social environment with this observation: the Eastern European "always remains an adolescent, governed by the sudden ebb and flow of inner chaos." (*Native Realm*, p. 67) The wording returns much later on in the book in an interesting manner. It is around 1950 and Miłosz is, by now, representing the People's Republic of Poland in Washington. He is looking for someone capable of discussing literature and can find only one candidate: the poet and diplomat, St. John Perse. "It seems I bored him terribly. The author of 'Anabasis', ensconced in his lofty solitude of a voluntary exile, looked upon the moral tempests and struggles of his contemporaries as one regards the ebb and flow of the sea." (*Native Realm*, p. 281) St. John Perse could, in other words, view history from an Olympian perspective while the Eastern European is a victim of tides. The Frenchman defines the world that the Eastern European is a marginal and exposed part of. (We remember that Miłosz' compatriot Gombrowicz tried to use his marginal position as an Argentinean exile as a resource for profiling himself in a judging and judgmental position).

From the beginning, Miłosz is, just as heterogeneous as his Wilna is but he is heading West and we are to meet him in Warsaw, Washington and Paris. Eventually, he considers himself a "Greek" (in roughly the same way as Nietzsche presented himself as a "Pole"). He summarizes his Europe like this:

> Poland and the Dordogne, Lithuania and Savoy, the narrow little streets in Wilno and the Quartier Latin, all fused together. I was like an ancient Greek. I had simply moved from one city to another. My native Europe, all of it, dwelled inside me, with its mountains, forests, and capitals; and that map of the heart left no room for my troubles. (*Native Realm*, p. 294)

This "map of the heart" is certainly not a sentimental map. Instead it has a historic and political dimension with the catastrophes of the Second World War as the indisputable center. In some intensive chapters Miłosz tells us about his escape in the beginning of the war, on foot, from Wilna to Warsaw. It is a piqarescue adventure told with macabre humor, full of appalling details, given in an odd mixture of distance and concreteness. Coming to war-time Warsaw was of course to jump out of the frying-pan into the fire: with relentless severity Miłosz tells us about the occupation, the uprising in the ghetto, the annihilation of the city. "Travelers who have visited Warsaw since the Second World War cannot imagine that on the same space a completely different city once stood." (*Native Realm*, p. 201)

Miłosz miraculously survived the war: "The four years I spent in Warsaw were no exception to the general rule, and every day was a gift that defied probability." (*Native Realm*, p. 231) From his remembering perspective he can present the surviving self as consequently and fatalistically disdainful when confronted with German and Russian occupants. He has a well-trained sense for the absurdities of existence, including an unsentimental but passionate love for what might be called the physics of survival: the adaptability of the body, the food that is easily accessible, things that do not change, like language and clandestine culture. Finally the image of the cosmopolite Eastern European Czesław Miłosz is such that he is exposed to the ebb and flow of history (but he can swim). He is constantly in love with a world in constant state of change, a good European in an evil part of Europe. When Miłosz constructs and presents himself as an Eastern European, it means that he is the incomplete but enduring result of a heterogeous and conflict-ridden culture with a catastrophic history.

*

Vladimir Nabokov is another Eastern European with exile and loss as decisive and thematic elements in his writing. Nabokov was brought up in an aristocratic setting and was compelled to leave Russia after the revolution. He was then 20 years of age and was to spend the following 20 years in a comparatively meager European exile in England, Germany and France. After leaving Europe for the USA in 1940, he started writing in English with considerable although late success. In other words, he was doubly exiled and changed language (although he states that his English preceded his Russian and that he could write in French just as well). He developed impressive writing in English as well as in Russian and not only literary; he also wrote with considerable expertise on butterflies and on chess. I shall restrict myself here to the autobiographical works that he started in the 1940s, which are published partly in journals and also as a book in 1951, entitled *Conclusive Evidence*. Nabokov later revised and extended this version and it was eventually published in 1967 as *Speak, Memory. An Autobiography Revisited*. In the intervening period, he penned a Russian version meaning that the result is — as he puts it in the preface — a "re-Englishing of a Russian re-version of what had been an English re-telling of Russian memories in the first place."[88] Nabokov was evidently motivated to take up life writing when his old life, connected to Russia and Europe, was lost. He continued to write of his old life for 20 years, practically his entire period as an American writer. The double exile, in combination with the new language, simply created the need to settle the accounts and the images of the old self.

Speak, Memory consists of 15 chapters that isolate thematic constellations and present them in significant images. Nabokov declares the construction of such themes to be "the true purpose of autobiography" (*Speak, Memory*, p. 23). More specifically, he calls it *thematic designs*, meaning thematic patterns as well as their construction. The "designer" of these themes seems to be a distinctive and solid subject. Irrespective of the fact that the writing took place over a very long period; he never allows us to doubt that he is in full control of his writing when he invites his memory to find and produce an "instantaneous and transparent organism of events, of which the poet (sitting in a lawn chair, at Ithaca, N.Y.) is the nucleus." (*Speak, Memory*, p. 169) The "poet" – Nabokov – is in all senses the subject ("nucleus") here, devoting himself to loving images from his early childhood up to the European exile and departure for the USA. He presents the book as "a systematically correlated assemblage of personal recollections" (*Speak, Memory*, p. 7); its system is not chronological however. Nabokov confesses that he does not believe in time but prefers to "fold" it in his working memory: "I like to fold my magic carpet, after use, in such a way as to superimpose one part of the pattern upon another. Let visitors trip." (*Speak, Memory*, p.109)

By this "folding," Nabokov tries to achieve a form of "timelessness." This creates an interesting tension in his biography. Like all biographies it has a chronology heading for the presence of writing; Nabokov maintains this chronology while going against it. The collector of butterflies confesses that "the highest enjoyment of timelessness — in a landscape selected at random — is when I stand among rare butterflies and their food plants." (*Speak, Memory*, p. 109) But all his commemorative images seek a similar perfection of timelessness: the mother kissing the Russian soil, the father being hoisted by

---

88   *Speak, Memory. An Autobiography Revisited.* Penguin Classics 2000, p. 10. Reference will be given in the text.

his peasants after affording them an advantage of sorts, the different governesses, the Summer residence, the teenage love, the first poetic inspiration, the meetings with Russians in Cambridge, Berlin, Paris. When Nabokov reveals his dislike of sleeping — "I simply cannot get used to the nightly betrayal of reason, humanity, genius" (*Speak, Memory*, p. 85) — you suspect this to be a resistance to the very passage of time, at least when it passes without his control. Yet when his memory has intervened and designed its images, he approaches the satisfaction of timelessness:

> A sense of security, of well-being, of summer warmth pervades my memory. That robust reality makes a ghost of the present. The mirror brims with brightness; a bumblebee has entered the room and bumps against the ceiling. Everything is as it should be, nothing will ever change, nobody will ever die. (*Speak, Memory*, p. 62)

The speaking memory, the memory invited to speak, that is of course the working memory of the writer, but it is also the forgotten phenomenon that is unearthed as a memory. Nabokov works in the spirit of Proust. He permits the tiny detail to carry a world at the same time as he is the magician designing this world. The memory is a kind of creative meeting between the two selves of life writing: the "poet" of the present, sitting in his American garden, meeting his past and almost forgotten self. The memory listens to the past and visualizes the past, it creates the past (or at least the images of the past). The memory balances between Now and Then and Nabokov barely gives his reader a chance to decide if it is Now or Then that takes the initiative in the work of his memory. The images we are shown seem distinctive and reliable, they convince us of their presence and their veracity. Still, Nabokov does not permit us to forget that it is his writing self that creates the images. It is the poet on his lawn in Ithaca that we actually meet in presence.

One chapter begins with an announcement from the "poet": "I am going to show a few slides, but first let me indicate the where and the when of the matter." (*Speak, Memory*, p. 120) Nabokov displays us his images, his "slides": he wants us to see. He recalls for instance on a "particular day that I see with the utmost clarity the sunspangled river" (*Speak, Memory*, p. 25); "I next see my mother leading me bedwards through the enormous hall" (*Speak, Memory*, p. 66); and, again, his mother: "There she is. I see so plainly her abundant dark hair, brushed up high and covertly graying." (*Speak, Memory*, p. 75) The images he sees are, of course, chosen and arranged according to the principles made up by the poetical memory artist of the present. This "poet" keeps reminding us of his existence, for instance when he presents the image of his first love: "Seen through the carefully wiped lenses of time, the beauty of her face is as near and as glowing as ever." (*Speak, Memory*, p. 178) Or when he pretends to be overwhelmed when remembering his teachers: "A bewildering sequence of English nurses and governesses, some of them wringing their hands, others smiling at me enigmatically, come out to meet me as I re-enter my past." (*Speak, Memory*, p. 68) Not without irony, he reminds us that he, the poet of presence, has the initiative, for instance when starting the story of an early romance like this: "I am now going to do something quite difficult, a kind of double somersault with a Welsh waggle (old acrobats will know what I mean), and I want complete silence, please." (*Speak, Memory*, p.159) He is essentially doing exactly that with all his images: he calls for our attention, then starts a show asking us to *see*. Sometimes it is with the accent on the poet of presence, sometimes on the child or young man that preceded him. Sometimes these are evenly matched, for instance in the passage on the first love just quoted, where Nabokov boasts having "carefully wiped [the] lenses of time." The result: the stable and timeless image of the past.

Nabokov's presentation of himself as a remembering and demonstrating "poet" in full control is perforated by his fascination for the timeless: every "timeless" image is a reminder of time past and of the passing time. He certainly does not neglect the demands of the genre for development. In the chapter on the father especially, he renders his portrait in strict chronological order from birth to death. When presenting himself, Nabokov heads for immortality but lands in this tense exchange between Now and Then, that is essential to life writing. Nabokov's strategy easily accommodates the great tradition of life writing. Nevertheless, his emphasis on showing images creates tensions that are equally due to the experiences of loss and departure made by the doubly exiled. Tensions are not only created by the temporal distance between Now and Then, but also by geographical, political and linguistic distance. Nabokov's Russia is gone forever. He is not sentimental about this fact. Instead, he ironizes over the Russian emigrants between the wars, "who imitated in foreign cities a dead civilization, the remote, almost legendary, almost Sumerian mirages of St. Petersburg and Moscow, 1900–1916." (*Speak, Memory*, p. 216). His Russian civilization is just as irrevocably lost as his childhood and this contributes, I assume, to his mapping ambition. When Nabokov invites his memory to "speak" it produces the images that, taken together, comprise a map of a lost kingdom as an imaginary recovery.

Nevertheless, the biographical impulse has its ambiguities: it recreates and recovers but at the same time cannot avoid emphasizing the distance to be bridged. Nabokov makes a virtue out of autobiographical necessity when using his memory to extend the temporal distance that he wants to bridge. The tension of this project means that it differs from classical autobiographies. Nabokov's modernity is due to the conditions of exile and can be read as irony. The phenomenon is evident in all his books and is thereby well known to Nabokov's readers. Here it perforates the remembering "poet" and the images he recalls. Irony surfaces, for instance, in the chapter on Russian emigrants when he starts praising the writer Sirin – Nabokov's own Russian signature; although, above all, is present in the final chapters when he starts addressing a Thou: his wife Véra. We understand that the presence, that constituted the starting-point for his autobiographical endeavor, is private and inaccessible to everyone other than the narrator and those closest to him. He does not ruin his own project with this manoeuvre. Instead he reminds us that his life writing — the writing of his past life as well as the life of the "poet" on his American lawn — is nothing but a beautiful construction. And that it could be nothing but a construction.

*

Elias Canetti was presented in the preceding chapter via his disturbing book *The Voices of Marrakesh*. This was a book of memory and written some time after the events chronicled (which he emphasizes in the subtitle "Notes after a journey"). Some years later, he went farther back in a life-writing endeavor. This developed into a classical autobiography, in the sense that Canetti begins his project facing the end of his life and writing at a great distance from the facts: he was born in 1905 and *The Tongue Set Free* came out in *1977, The Torch in My Ear* in 1980, *The Play of the Eye* in 1985.[89] There is also a fourth,

---

89   *Die gerettete Zunge, Die Fackel im Ohr, Das Augenspiel*. Transl. by Joachim Neugroschel (I-II) and Ralph Manheim (III), published in one volume, New York: Farrar, Straus and Giroux 1999. Reference will be given in the text.

unfinished part, published posthumously: *Party im Blitz* (2003). The subtitles talk about "the story of my youth" and "the story of my life": the books start in childhood and follow the chronology of his life. It is, in other words, a vast and apparently conventional autobiography. However it is "modernized" by Canetti's remarkable use of memory and of the thematic structure that the titles allude to: tongue, ear, eye.

Canetti makes no secret about the long distance between his writing self and the life he is writing about. We frequently read reminders such as: "I still feel the tension in the back of my neck as I tried to view its entire length." (p. 24) – this is his memory of seeing a comet in the sky 60 years earlier. Another example is when he remembers and credits a riot in Vienna as providing the decisive impulse for his lifework *Masse und Macht*: "Fifty-three years have passed, and the agitation of that day is still in my bones." (p. 484) It is evident too, when he tells us about some people he met at a musical gathering in 1933: "My impression of these people were indelible; I never saw most of them again, yet now, fifty years later, I can recall them clearly to mind." (p. 648)

Reminders like these do not, however, explain why he is writing his life or why he writes the way he does: in separate episodes isolating certain events and people. Although the episodes are chronologically arranged; they cannot be said to establish a continuity, instead they *jump* from one episode to the other. Accordingly they omit a number of events from his personal and public career, events that would have been obligatory in a conventional autobiography. Canetti tells us about his life but gives us no CV or even a continuity. He *conceals* just as much as he shows, a phenomenon observed by Claudio Magris:

> Canetti is the great poet of transformation also in his autobiography, that conceals him and seems to cover him. ... Behind the obliging suppleness of this autobiography, that ... in a disappointing way seems to say it all, there is a winding reservation that conceals an unknown other-ness, an identity that cannot be grasped or imagined.[90]

The quotation comes from an anthology devoted to Canetti's writing, *Hüter der Verwandlung*. Its title – *Guardian of Transformation* – comes from one of Canetti's aphorisms in *Die Provinz der Menschen* from 1973. *Transformation* is also a key concept when Canetti writes his own life, for instance when he remembers how an early

---

90 *Hüter der Verwandlung*, München: Hanser 1985, p. 272. My transl.

experience of reading the *Odyssey* and Ulysses gave him "a complete and very substantial model, presenting itself in many forms [Verwandlungen]. (p. 103) Or when he remembers being impressed by the actor Ludwig Hardt: his flexible voice taught him something about the "metamorphosis, which preoccupied me more and more." (p. 524) Magri's observation does not imply that Canetti was writing an "inner" biography, nor does it that he kept changing form and fashion. It means rather that Canetti presents and remembers himself as consisting of ripe and full memories but also of unwritten and unknown gaps. That is a structure that has occurred to Canetti himself, judging from several passages where he talks about *eine Fremdheit*, an estrangement also from himself.

Canetti's transformations can also be understood sociologically and structurally: a permanent change of geographical and social positions. Already in the first part, the setting switches from Bulgarian Ruse to Manchester, Vienna and Zurich. The second part adds Frankfurt and Berlin to the list; while the third keeps mainly to Vienna. The languages also keep changing, not the German that we read but the languages followed by Canetti: from the Spanish-Jewish Ladino spoken by the family in Ruse, combined with Bulgarian in the household and Hebrew and French at school, into English, then the German of Vienna and of Switzerland, competing with *Hochdeutsch* [High/Standard German]. In the fourth, unfinished part English returns. The death of his father comes early on in the first part, like a caesura that determines a geographical and social transformation. In the second part, he commutes between Vienna and Berlin; while the third, taking place in Vienna, culminates with the death of his mother — in Paris. Loss and exile determine his life story and his life writing in much the same way as with Nabokov. Canetti demonstrates the Diaspora that is due to a Spanish-Bulgarian Jew on his itinerary through Europe and history — and perhaps paradigmatic for a European intellectual during the 20th century. A final departure comes after the unfinished fourth part: from England, Canetti moved back to Zurich – and I imagine that this return, together with approaching death, motivated this great work of memory.

Death is a prominent theme in these books, in contrast to the vital forces used in the titles: tongue, ear, eye. In an introductory chapter, he arrives at this conclusion: "There is almost nothing bad that I couldn't say about humans and humankind. And yet my pride in them is so great that there is only one thing I really hate: their enemy, death." (p. 9) The individual death that was of the greatest importance was that of the father, which happened when Elias was no more than seven years old. Nevertheless he remembers it in graphic detail more than 60 years on. Above all, he remembers the reaction of the mother: her desperate screaming "right out". The book about the tongue is emblematically concentrated in this living scream against final death.

Memory is the faculty whereby Canetti conquers death. This may sound pompous but it corresponds with his intentions as well as with the immediate reader-impression of a memory-artist giving life to long past events. For Canetti, just as much as for Proust, memorial writing is waking the dead and all that is dead and then keeping them and it alive. Memory potentiates alive and, in the second part, Canetti confesses his faith in this faculty: "I bow to memory, every person's memory." This is at the same time as he declares his "disgust" towards anyone permitting himself "a beauty operation on a memory." (p. 534) Canetti, the memory-artist, gives life to episodes, events, images and above all to human beings that he has met: his autobiography is just as much a portrait galley as it is a self portrait. As an intriguing example of his ambitions, I can mention the portrait of Alban Berg in the third part. It is a short chapter about a person who had little importance for Canetti but he wants to tell us about his widow Helene, whom he meets 30 years after the death of her husband and quotes as: "Ah, Herr C.! That was a long time ago. Alban still speaks of you." The widow has the habit of talking with her dead husband and Canetti comments: "It takes a great deal of love to create a dead man who never dies, to listen to him and to speak to him, to find out his wishes, which he will always have because one has created him." (p. 763)

Canetti thereby characterizes not only the widow but also the life-giving ambition that triggers his own memorial work. The ambivalence of this work emanates from the fact that his portraits not only give life but that, in giving life, they also fixate the people portrayed and in a sense kill them, or rather: mummify them. I am not saying that Canetti is committing that which he finds "disgusting": manipulating his memory. Rather, the impression given is one of merciless honesty, an impression that is modified by all the gaps and lacunae that allow alternative interpretations and stories. Canetti is certainly not unfamiliar with this possibility. He demonstrates it in an anecdotal fashion in the second part where he meets a cousin that we remember from the first part: Elias wanted to attack her with an axe and she has him scalded. Now the cousin is dismissing this episode: "You just imagined it." (p. 366) We believe that she is the one who adjusts her memory but Canetti opens up the possibility that his own work of memory is infiltrated by imagination, wishful thinking and construction.

The ambivalence of his portrayals becomes striking in portraits that are negative in one aspect or another. For example of the critical portrait of Brecht and Berlin in the second part, the scornful portrait of Alma Mahler in the third part and especially the aggressive portrait of Iris Murdoch in *Party im Blitz*. The latter is only explicable if we regard it as a sketch: we are in the preliminary phase of what could have become a fourth part. It makes you wonder about the aggressions that have been polished away in the finished parts. In other words, reading the unfinished fourth part means that the charming character of spontaneous flow gives way to an impression of construction and reconstruction.

The three finished parts impart an exceptional portrait of Canetti's mother: devoted, sacrificing, proud, demanding, critical, despotic. The ambivalence that pervades the portrait of the mother is also the ambivalence of memorial writing: it brings to life and it preserves and it mummifies. This sits well with the many transformations in which Canetti writes himself: they make up a constant and consistent figure that is incessantly on the move. The "life work", that he finds out about in 1925, is not completed until the publication of *Masse und Macht* some thity-five years later. Let us say that he was prepared to start his *real* life work after that: to conquer death with his memory. The result is one of the great autobiographies, not least because of its highly developed ambivalence, its transformations, its play between showing and concealing – Canetti is not only writing about himself and writing himself but he is also writing a continuous commentary on the very impossibility of his own project.

*

Michael Ondaatje is often called a "post-colonial" writer. The reason for this is his "multi-cultural" background: his schooling and his writing in English, although his childhood was in Ceylon and adult life in Canada. Colonialism is only indirectly present in the autobiographical rhapsody he published in 1982: *Running in the Family*.

Ondaatje was 5–6 years old when Ceylon became independent in 1948 (renamed Sri Lanka in 1972). In his book, there are few political events and a great deal more family drama. There are also some hints of the Dutch background to the family, going back to the time before the English colonization.

Ondaatje demonstrates a highly original play between *showing*, *searching* and *concealing* that is witty, sad and poetical. *Running in the Family* is neither a conventional autobiography nor a self-portrait. Rather it is an organized literary visit to and through the family archive and memories of his childhood – Ondaatje spent his first 11 years on Ceylon. The structure is given by two return journeys from Canada, Ondaatje visiting remaining family and refreshing his memory. *The journey back* is a mythical and traumatic gesture among life writers. Ondaatje starts his journey with the sudden insight that he is making his journey back to meet the family that he has outgrown and that he now wants to approach via the route that remains available to him: through literature. "I wanted to touch them into words."[91] He is *searching* his own background and adolescence and he also wants to *show* his family, his history, his environment. He is writing his life in an indirect way: as a result of the family and environment described, or as a part of it, or as an effort to harmonize all those eccentric and picturesque, and at times demonic, components that we are invited to meet. In a final footnote, Ondaatje credits all the people that he thanks for information and he admits that the names create an impression of authenticity. Still, he does not want to call his book a *history* but instead a *portrait* or a *gesture* (*Running in the Family*, p. 206). The last term strikes me as accurate when naming what Ondaatje does: a visit in his childhood that is also an intervention and a memorial work in order to dig up and reconstruct the self and the life that is concealed in his own background.

I would call about half of the text hymnic: it consists of poems and prose poems that celebrate the Ceylon of his childhood; especially the heat, the monsoon, the vegetation, the insects, the snakes. These pieces are layered with family memories that range from straightforward information to tall stories and myth. Here, we encounter a succession of picturesque ancestors and on occasion the impressions from actual meetings made in Ceylon also, where Ondaatje

---

91 *Running in the Family*, Toronto: McClellan & Stewart 1983 (1982), p. 22. Reference will be given in the text.

searches for information and corroborating memories, most of them concerning his parents. Both in the beginning of the book and towards the end he inserts some photographs of the parents: in the beginning of the book, two separate photographs of two beautiful youngsters, on the road to becoming a couple (even if we suspect the worst after some of the anecdotes describing the father's debauchery at Cambridge). At the end of the book (*Running in the Family*, p. 163), he adds another photography, this time showing the parents together: they are still young and they pull violent and comical faces at each other. Ondaatje assures us that this is the only existing photo of the parents within the same frame and that the father has written on the back of the photo that it depicts "what we think of married life." In fact the entire book culminates in a portrait of the parents, particularly the father.

Drinking is the most striking theme of the book, besides the monsoon and the landscape. From the beginning, Ondaatje recounts disturbing anecdotes concerning individuals and distant relatives that are either drinking in a civilized way or drinking themselves to death. This custom meanders through the generations and culminates in the father, who is gradually presented as an alcoholic on a grand scale. During certain periods, he is a compulsive drinker with no regard for consequences and becomes involved in adventures that may be transformed into anecdotes but that can also seem desperate and destructive. Inevitably it ends with the dissolution of the marriage and the family, finally with the death of the father. The book even starts in drinking: Ondaatje describes himself as highly intoxicated when he decides to follow the traces of his family to see what is "running in the family." And he ends it by approaching his father or even *becoming* his drinking father in a gesture of literary empathy.

When Ondaatje makes this "gesture" it means that he remembers and that he evokes his conditions, his background, his environment. In this process he is also approaching himself, showing and writing himself.

*

Finally, in this cavalcade, come two writers that seem to oppose the basic observation of this chapter: exile and loss as decisive components in modern life writing. As far as I know, the Austrian *Thomas Bernhard* lived his entire life in his affectionately hated Austria (except for a few adolescent years in Germany) and most of his writing sticks to this setting. The Turk *Orhan Pamuk* claims to have lived and worked his whole life in Istanbul and most of his writing takes place in Istanbul and Turkey. Nevertheless, these two writers demonstrate new versions of life writing that are not unaffected by the modern predicament of exile and loss.

Thomas Bernhard enters what might be called an *inner exile* when he continually furiously lashes out at his country and its morality and politics and customs from the inside. His perspective oscillates between knowing-from-within and critizising-from-the-outside in a manner that also distinguishes his literary life writing. Bernhard wrote no less than five titles in an autobiography that deals with his childhood and adolescence and ends up with *A Child (Ein Kind* 1982). As ever with Bernhard, it is a matter of compact, intense and manic texts so to speak: an in-depth-study of the childhood environment, confrontations with wrongs that have not been forgotten, diatribes against Austrian miseries. Towards the end of *Ein Kind*, Berhard revisits the sites of "my deepest despair"[92] — a home for "vicious" children where he had to spend some time — and the whole autobiographical suite has exactly this character: Bernhard goes back to the places and people and situations that have once caused him to suffer and continue to cause him pain.

From my present perspective, the novel *Extinction (Auslöschung. Ein Zerfall* 1986) is yet more interesting. It is Bernhard's last major work, 650 pages, not one new paragraph, two huge blocks of compact prose. First, a monologue of the first person narrator, Murau, standing in his apartment in Rome surveying family photos following the news of the sudden death of his parents and brother. Then, another monologue in Wolfsegg: the location where the narrator attends the funeral, also the place of his Austrian life. Wolfsegg seems to be a summary of everything that the narrator hates in Austria and wants to dissociate himself from by living in Italy. We follow an obtrusive narrator addressing us and writing his own life although this is not Bernhard's life but the fictitious Murau. There are some notable breaks from fiction: Wolfsegg is an authentic place and a tiny parenthesis on the last page tells us that Murau passed away shortly after his life story was finished. Accordingly we are invited to

---

92   *Ein Kind*, Salzburg: Residenz, 1982, p. 146.

imagine Bernhard as the discreet editor-publisher of the manuscript that Murau left behind.

Murau does not have much good to say about his family or his childhood and adolescence in Wolfsegg. But he has all the more to critizise in the sharpest possible way and according to what he calls the "art of exaggeration," [*Übertreibungskunst*]. This "art" is his most important means to "endure existence" and he calls it the very key to the arts, philosophy and all spiritual activity.[93] It is easy to imagine that Bernhard uses Murau as a megaphone to announce those exaggerations that make existence endurable for himself also; and to pronounce those incisive truths that are normally kept silent. Only one member of the family is tolerated in Murau's memorial work: an uncle who set an example by leaving Wolfsegg and Austria. The uncle not only managed to do that, he was also rumored to have written a *Antiautobiographie*, a manuscript that was unfortunately lost after his death. Clearly it is easy to imagine that Bernhard uses Murau's autobiographical work in order to write a kind of *Antiautobiographie*.

An interesting theme in this eruptive book is photography. As mentioned previously, the monologue of the first part is motivated by Murau looking at some family photos. He regards his father and mother and brother and sisters as reproduced in ways that he finds utterly misleading and false. Moreover he does not hesitate to exaggerate a crushing criticism of photos in general, a criticism that also hits out at modern civilization since this is, according to Murau, attached to photography. Humanity "clings to photography" (*Auslöschung*, p.128), photography is the "work of the devil of our time" (*Auslöschung*, p. 243), photography is the greatest "scorn" imaginable, "the greatest scorn of the world," [*die allergrößte Weltverhöhnung*]. (*Auslöschung*, p. 252) Photography initiated "a general state of ignorance" (*Auslöschung*, p. 646) culminating with moving images. (It is not difficult to imagine what Murau would have to say about the current digitalization of photography).

There seem to be two reasons for this condemnation of photography. First: the photography only shows "the grotesque and comical moment", not the human being "throughout life", [*zeitlebens*]. Therefore, photography is "an unheard-of falsification of nature, base and inhuman." (*Auslöschung*, p. 26f.) Second: the photography

---

93 *Auslöschung: Ein Zerfall*. Frankfurt: Suhrkamp 1996 (1986), p. 612. Reference will be given in the text.

does not exaggerate. It shows the moment but it does not show how moments connect and Bernhard's and Murau's exaggerations aim to show connections.

To reiterate, the deprecation of photography occurs while Murau is looking at his family photographs. The situation is certainly not unusual in life writing. We have already seen an elegant version in Nabokov's memorial work: "I am going to show a few slides". I shall soon come to Orhan Pamuk's extensive use of photographs in his memorial work and in my final chapter I shall discuss W. G. Sebald's use of photographs in his life writing (which is all the more interesting here since Sebald's prose seems to be influenced by Bernhard: in syntactical and critical respects). I do not know of anyone (after Baudelaire) other than Bernhard's Murau who violently dissociates himself from photography and I imagine that Bernhard's criticism is part of his ambition to write an *Antiautobiographie*. I think we have to admit that his exaggerated criticism reveals something indisputable: photography catches the moment but lacks the continuity, transformations and temporality of life and narrative. Roland Barthes makes similar points in his famous meditation of photography in *La chambre claire* (1980) — although his conclusion is the opposite: that the photography can only remind of death.

What, then, is the connection that Bernhard allows Murau to discover and that photography cannot discern? A possible answer to this question is already in the title of the book: it concerns an annihilating *Auslöschung*, an extinction that the photography seems to contest. Another, most probably related, answer appears later on in the book, when Murau approaches the house of his childhood, *die Kindervilla*, meaning that he tries to enter his very childhood, *die Kindheit*. This approach triggers a meditation where over several pages Murau insists that we can only find a "gaping void," [*eine gähnende Leere*], when searching for our childhood. This phrase of void is called both "famous" and "notorious" and is repeated in italics for emphasis roughly ten times over a couple of pages. (*Auslöschung*, p. 598ff.) I would think that this "famous" void is connected to time: the childhood has definitely passed and cannot be recalled — and the same is true for any phase of life. The effort of life writing is doomed to failure when it is regarded as an endeavor to awaken the past and bring it to life. Not only that: the life writing effort cannot but confirm the distance to the life that was and to living life and must therefore function as a death sentence.

Such is the logic that I imagine governs the exaggerations that Berhard causes Murau to develop. Such is the *Auslöschung* ignored by photography but resisted and confirmed by Murau. My own reflection is that Bernhard exaggerates the doubling that I have found to be constitutive for the life writing tradition: the distance and doubling between the remembering writer and the one that once lived and is still alive. Bernhard has turned the classical motivation for autobiography upside down: if imminent death motivated the work of memory then – for Bernhard, or Bernhard's Murau – it is the memorial work that motivates "extinction" and death. Bernhard's *Antiautobiography* is therefore a critical commentary to the whole tradition of life writing. It also allows for the suspicion that Bernhard uses Murau's exaggerations in order to write his life.

*

Orhan Pamuk has often given his work of fiction a personal signature. In *My Name is Red* (*Benim Adim Kirmizi* 1998) there is an Orhan: the youngest member of a family comprising a mother with numerous admirers, two sons and an absent husband and father. Towards the end of the book, the very same Orhan is transformed into its writer. In this crafty manner, Pamuk comments on the thematics of the book: it deals with Turkish miniature painters from the 16th century embroiled in a conflict between traditionalists and innovators. The innovation consists precisely of making a subjective perspective and even a signature part of the picture. *Istanbul* (2003) is not a work of fiction: the subtitle is "memories of a city", it is a work of memorial life. Here we meet with Pamuk's own family, much like the family presented in the novel. In *Snow* (*Kar* 2002) Orhan turns up again, now as an editor of the story told by the main character, a Turkish exile poet. But it is in *Istanbul* that Pamuk himself is the main character or rather the mediator relating his own story to the story of the family and the city. It handles the interplay between Orhan Pamuk and his city, the identity of the city as reflected by Orhan, the identity of Orhan as conditioned by the city, as a part of the identity of the city. Towards the end of the book he makes a simple yet unavoidable observation: the city looked sad while he was sad himself. Or was it the melancholy of the city that influenced him?

The relationship is mutual: "I poured my soul in the city's streets and there it still resides."[94]

As previously mentioned, Pamuk claims to have lived his whole life in Istanbul, in the same block and, for most of the time, in the same house. While this probably held some poetic truth at the time of writing, the situation has changed. Pamuk's writing has always mediated: between himself and the city, between East and West, between tradition and innovation. In a political situation dominated by extremes, the role of the mediator has apparently become a provocation and Pamuk has been forced to exile. In *Istanbul* he claims to already be exiled although still living in the city. He even claims that everyone living in Istanbul is exiled: "Istanbul is a place where, for the past hundred and fifty years, no one has been able to feel completely at home." (*Istanbul*, p. 103)

This has to do with the breakdown of the Ottoman Empire, and also with the enduring conflict between East and West, a conflict that seems to be inscribed in the very topography and geography of the city. On several occasions, Pamuk returns to riots in the 1950s: these resembled pogroms and ethnical purges, whereby Greek and Armenian shops and flats were sacked. The riots form a childhood memory signifying a major tendency in the modern history of Turkey. The emergence of the national state after the disintegration of the Ottoman Empire connotes a turn to the West. Yet it also means an exclusion of the ethnic and linguistic plurality. Not only Armenians and Greeks, but also Jews and Kurds were oppressed for nationalistic reasons according to a pattern that is far too well known in the modern history of Europe and the Middle East. Pamuk: "It was an end of the grand polyglot, multicultural Istanbul of the imperial age; the city stagnated, emptied itself out, and became a monotonous, monolingual town in black and white." (*Istanbul*, p. 215)

This loss triggers the form of melancholy that Pamuk names *hüsün* and describes as greater than an individual affectation. Instead it is a kind of communal melancholy that covers the city and the Bosporus as a fog, "so dense that you can almost touch it, almost see it spread like a film over its people and its landscapes." (*Istanbul*, p. 89) The book holds a very rich photographic documentation of historic Istanbul and the photographs emphasize the melancholy:

---

94 *Istanbul*, transl. Maureen Freely, London: Faber & Faber 2005, p. 313. Reference will be given in the text.

empty streets and bridges, decaying wooden houses suggest the loss of former greatness. In addition, black and white photographs from Pamuk's family album suggest the loss of a united and happy family. (The photos seem to confirm the criticism of Bernhard-Murau: they simulate a life but they signify loss and death. However, the photos also function according to W. G. Sebald's use of photos: as reminders of lost life and as invitations to memorial work, this will be discussed in my final chapter.)

Pamuk calls attention to the many Western visitors that have been fascinated and irritated by Istanbul: from Nerval to Hamsun. He claims to be grateful to Théophile Gautier, who roamed the city in the middle of the 19th century dressed as a Muslim in order to register his fascination undisturbed. With their help, Pamuk writes, the inhabitant of Istanbul has learnt to see himself and his city with a double perspective, with an Eastern gaze as well as a Western one. I would like to add that at least Pamuk has learned exactly that about himself. This means that he can inform his fellow compatriots from a Western perspective and he can inform us Western readers from an Eastern perspective. The price to pay for this is the melancholy that is determined by not being quite at home anywhere. Pamuk claims to have lived at the same spot, in the same city his whole life. Still, he appears to be the most homeless and exiled in the gallery of writers that have been presented in this chapter, all of them showing the way – or the ways – to the prose of modern life. Exile and loss make the modern conditions of what Hegel called "the prose of reality."[95] A prose working on the borderline between life and writing forms the answer.

---

95 *Werke* 14, Frankfurt: Suhrkamp 1970, p. 219.

IV Extensions

Sebald's photographic prose

What happens to the fictional character of the literary text when it is interrupted and infiltrated by photographic images? What happens to prose when it becomes visual?[96]

My starting-point for these questions has been the writings of W. G. Sebald and his frequent and original use of photographs. But the questions were touched upon already in chapter 7. I observed earlier that Orhan Pamuk's many photographs in *Istanbul* operate as "reminders of lost life and as invitations to memorial work". I also pondered on Thomas Bernhard's way of having his character, Murnau, scorn photography as the "work of the devil of our time" – while intensely observing photography.

There is, of course, nothing remarkable in using photographs in an autobiography. The autobiographical image underlines the claims for reality and verifies the past that the autobiographer remembers from the presence of his or her writing position. The image can be called a support for memory or a function of memory demonstrating the temporal exchange between now and then that is the precondition of autobiography. Hence Vladimir Nabokov in *Speak, Memory* (1967) when about to start an episode: "I am going to show a few slides." Nabokov also includes a couple of photographs but does not appear to slip into fiction. The first modern example of photographic intervention in fictional text is probably Georges Rodenbach's novel *Bruges-la-mort* (1892), including an array of street photos from Bruges (Brügge), most of them showing house façades and only one of them showing human beings. The reason for this was probably a technical one but the result emphasized the theme of the book. This was based on the popular myth of Bruges as

---

96 I am indebted to Marius Wulfsberg and his chapter "On Phototextuality" when discussing these questions. See *Aesthetics at Work* (my edition, Oslo: Unipub 2007). I am also reworking parts from my own essay in the same volume.

a "dead" town, coordinated by Rodenbach with a topical plot about a lonely man being haunted by a *femme fatale*, whom is mysteriously connected with the narrow streets of the town and with death. The photographs converge with the fiction while imparting an uncanny touch of death and reality.

More advanced examples arise in the heyday of modernism and surrealism. In 1928 Virginia Woolf's *Orlando* and André Breton's *Nadja* were published, both using photos although in quite different ways. Woolf's novel about the androgynous Orlando's adventures throughout many centuries may be read as a parody of biography, albeit with some "serious" touches. The text is interrupted by a set of photographs that underline the parody: the photos are supposed to be related to the different historical epochs described in the book and they are either taken directly from Vita Sackwille-West's family album or portray Vita herself (who was the model for Orlando) posing in different costumes. Interestingly, these photos were removed from later editions, probably in an attempt to emphasize the "serious" dimensions of the novel (although they return in some editions from the 1990s).

Breton continued to revise his *Nadja* until the final edition in 1963. Here, Breton tries to mythologize his meeting with the elusive Nadja, although it involves a meeting that is presented as authentic and a woman who exists not only in the text. We meet her gaze in a photo-montage (that only appeared in the final edition) and she is said to have contributed the childish drawings to the book (that are supposed to illustrate her mental state). She is also given at least one line of words, addressing the writer in a fashion that shows the literary construction at work: "André? André? ... You are about to write a novel about me."[97] Whether or not André really writes a "novel" is a matter of opinion : the text could also be termed a biographical *rêverie*, an array of memorial fragments with documentary pretensions. The photographs by Man Ray give the text a surrealistic flavor, while other photos are the simple documentation of addresses and locations mentioned in the text. In a preface to the final edition, Breton informs us that the photographs, along with *l'observation médicale* of Nadja's mental metamorphoses, are the principles *anti-littéraire* of the book. The photographs are supposed to eliminate

---

97   André Breton, *Nadja,* Paris: Gallimard 1998 (1964), p. 100. "André? André? ... Tu écriras un roman sur moi."

toute description and give the impression that the text is *pris sur le vif*, meaning that Breton claims to give us instant pictures, *snapshots*, of a reality that really was real.

W. G. Sebald, whom provided the starting-point for this extension, also problematizes literature as fiction and his extensive use of photographs contributes to this. He inaugurates this strategy in *Vertigo* (*Schwindel. Gefühle* 1990), where he mixes two texts of literary criticism and anecdote, on Stendhal and Kafka, with two autobiographical stories; all four are documented through photographs of train-tickets, hotel and restaurant bills, passport photos and so on. Also, his next book, *The Emigrants* (*Die Ausgewanderten* 1992), consists of four texts and Sebald fully develops his literary strategy here: he starts from an autobiographical perspective that merges with a portrait of a character that the narrator has met or known. This character is portrayed in a mixture of identification and reconstruction; the narrator traces the character's complicated and elusive history, going back to the black spots of European history from the 20th century, of which there is no shortage. The form is seemingly a documentary one: interviews, diary notes, letters, travels, research; all of this fused in a text that is interfoliated by black and white photographs. The last chapter of the book is characteristic: here, Sebald recalls his first visit to England and Manchester, his meeting with the painter Max Aurach, and also subsequent meetings with the same man, who is gradually foregrounded and whom eventually hands over his family album of photographs to the narrator. The person and name Aurach seems to be an elliptical version of the actual painter Frank Auerbach, while "Max" is the nickname that Sebald used with friends. (In the English edition, the name was changed in order to distance it from Auerbach). In this way, Sebald merges his fiction with reality and adds his signature to the picture so to speak. The painting presented in a photograph as made by Aurach is certainly close to paintings actually made by Auerbach. (Maybe it is an Auerbach; Sebald never references his photographs so we cannot make out their origin).

Sebald continues to develop this quasi-documentary strategy in his "English pilgrimage" *Rings of Saturn* (*Die Ringe des Saturn* 1995) and in the book that was to be his last, *Austerlitz* (2001) and the first to be called a "novel". Both contain a number of black-and-white photographs, including some that are said to portray the fictional character Austerlitz as a child and schoolboy; despite this (or perhaps because of it) the reader feels unsure about his status: who is it looking at us in the photos that are said to be of Jacques Austerlitz? Could it be Sebald himself, who has found some pictures from his childhood and youth?

In other words: the reader does not know if the novel *Austerlitz* is meant to be an autobiographical project. Perhaps it is an imaginary construction portraying a novelistic character, whom is mainly searching his own biography and history. The extensive use of photographic documentation invites us to regard even the novel *Austerlitz* as non-fictional; but we are also led to suspect that Sebald develops his own autobiographical project through a more or less fictitious autobiographical project. Sebald (or the publisher) calling this book a "novel" certainly does not put a stop to the problematization of fiction assisted by photos. Between *Rings of Saturn* and *Austerlitz*, he also published two books that were not designed as fiction but are made according to the same strategy as the explicitly literary books: a mixture of text and picture, autobiographical fragments merged with a critical presentation of a character or a phenomenon. I am thinking of *Logis in einem Landhaus*, a collection of literary criticism from 1998, and *Luftkrieg und Literatur* from 1999: afterthoughts on his lectures on the grand theme of Germany during World War II. The political essays insist on the priority of a documentary presentation, while the literary essays indulge in biographical anecdote; just as with those books that are closer to fiction, Sebald tries to merge biography and history. One essay is called "To the memory of Robert Walser", who is portrayed through a number of photos which punctuate a text that includes the following passage, where I think that Sebald implies himself:

> Walser himself once said that he is actually always writing the same novel, from one piece of prose to the other, a novel that could be characterized as a "in many ways disrupted and disseminated book of myself". One must add that the main character, the I, in this book of I myself, is hardly ever to be seen, but is rather spread out or hidden among all the others passing by.[98]

As an analogy to this, we can imagine Sebald himself as "hidden" in his own text, as "spread out" among his more or less fictitious characters in roughly the same way as his character Jacques Austerlitz. Austerlitz functions as a ghost in his own novel, or, to use the more

---

98 *Logis in einem Landhaus*, Fischer 2000 (1998), p. 147.

apt French word, a *revenant*, someone who keeps coming back: he is turning up unexpectedly and without evident reason at unpredictable junctures and settings. Sebald's application of black-and-white photographs emphasizes a kind of *revenant*-motive. That is also the case when he occasionally inserts a picture of himself: in *Vertigo* as a photograph of an outdated passport photo, in *Rings of Saturn* standing at the foot of a Lebanese cedar, "still not knowing about the ungood things that since have passed".[99] In a picture in *Austerlitz*[100] we see a foggy shop window with the photographer vaguely reflected: W.G. Sebald himself as a ghost.[101]

The epistemological situation becomes even more complicated when we come to those photographs in *Austerlitz* that are said to portray the main character as a boy, pictures that emphasize the ambivalence of both pictures and character. A photograph of a fictional character seems to inherently be a contradiction in terms; in this case, the fictional character Jacques Austerlitz cannot know for certain if it is indeed himself that he sees in the photo. So how are we to know?

Jacques Austerlitz is presented as a collector of photographs showing excerpts from his family album to his narrator. For both – for the narrator and his character – the pictorial interest is participating in the work of memory aiming to reconstruct the past. The photographs themselves are seldom remarkable, often unfocused and vague, and this amateurish touch strengthens the documentary effect and the ghostly character. According to the analysis of Mark M. Anderson, they "seem to come from nowhere, serving not as illustration of the text but as a slightly out-of-sync counterpoint, a kind of punctuation that subtly irritates and challenges our notion of what is real, what is fictional."[102] When Jacques Austerlitz researches his own past, he describes his work as an arrangement of photographs: "I began to assemble and recast anything that still passed muster in order to re-create before my eyes, as if in the pages of an album, the

---

99 *Die Ringe des Saturn*, Fischer 1997 (1995), p. 313.
100 *Austerlitz*, transl. Anthea Bell, Penguin 2002, p. 276. Reference will be given in the text.
101 I borrow this example from an article by Andrea Gnam in *Verschiebebahnhöfe der Erinnerung. Zum Werk W. G. Sebalds*, ed. Martin & Wintermann, Königshausen & Neumann 2007.
102 Mark M. Anderson, "The Edge of Darkness: On W. G. Sebald." *October* 106, Fall 2003, p. 109.

picture of the landscape, now almost immersed in oblivion, through which my journey had taken me." (*Austerlitz*, p. 171)

When Austerliz finds a photo of himself as a child he feels "the piercing, inquiring gaze" that he imagines is seen in the eyes of the boy. (*Austerlitz*, p. 260). Being pierced, *durchdrungen*, is actually a recurrent term used to describe the effect of the gaze that seems to emanate from the old photo: "As far back as I can remember, said Austerlitz, I have always felt as if I had no place in reality, as if I were not there at all, and never have I had this impression more strongly than on that evening in the Šporkova when the eyes of the Rose Queen's page pierced me.[103] The picture commented upon shows – perhaps – the boy Austerlitz dressed up like a page and it is also used on the cover of the book.

One suspects Roland Barthes in the background with his famous distinction between *studium* and *punctum* in his book on photography, *La chambre claire* (1980) – Sebald actually refers to Barthes in an interview from 1999 concerning his relation to photographs.[104] Barthes' *punctum* has to do with the appeal of the photograph, the expressive detail, the gaze that "jumps out" of the picture so to speak (and makes Jacques Austerlitz feel "pierced"). When the photograph is situated in a text, the documentary character is strengthened but also curiously displaced. The photograph hovers between fiction and documentation, it does not quite belong to an imaginary realm (of death), nor does it to any evident reality. Rather, the photograph shows us a *revenant* and its *"punctum"* reminds us of past reality while demanding new reality.

"My medium is prose, not the novel." Thus spoke W. G. Sebald in an interview from 1993.[105] Sebald executes the tendency of prose and prosification in all possible ways, not least in his only novel, *Austerlitz*. His extensive use of pictures underlines this tendency by their meticulous integration in the texts, making them continuous and compact. However, the pictures also emphasize the very contingency, that is the reality of prose as well as the prose of reality. Photographs install a hovering element, shifting between the now and then of historical presence and fictional invention. It may well

---

103   *Austerlitz*, p. 261. Transl. modified. The German has "als mich der Blick des Pagen der Rosenkönigin durchdrang."
104   According to Heiner Boehncke, "Clair obscur. W.G. Sebalds Bilder." In *Text + Kritik* 158, April 2003, p. 55.
105   In *Campo Santo*, München: Hanser 2003, p. 263.

be that Sebald's use of photos is already antiquated: the digitalization of the photographic medium possibly weakens the historical there-and-then of the traditional photograph. Alternatively, Sebald's ghost-like effects remind us of the possibilities of memorial work while approaching a situation where history is pure presence.

Human design

The literary presentation of the self was the concern of chapter 7 but the aesthetic and prosaic aspects of the self were already prominent in my two examples of the classics: Montaigne and Nietzsche. A vital reason for Montaigne embarking upon his essayistic project was the wish to go public with a portrait of himself; he wanted to "paint a portrait" and one could regard Montaigne as the literary version of the art of the self-portrait as it started in the Renaissance. Nietzsche experimented with a hyperbolic self-portrait in *Ecce homo* and in several earlier works he discussed and criticized the idea of the self. The tendency in this critique goes against any substantial view of the self and propagates a version of the human self as undefined and unfinished, as a dramatic structure with an aesthetic profile. In *The Gay Science*, Nietzsche imagines existence itself to be an aesthetic phenomenon and, "as an aesthetical phenomenon existence is still *bearable* to us."[106] Furthermore, the arts can teach us to "make such a phenomenon of ourselves". The idea is set forth later in the same book, under the heading *"What one should learn from the artist."* (Nr. 299) The artist is praised for his capacity to model and beautify reality. According to Nietzsche, we should learn from this; not in order to create works of art but in order to create our lives. The artists may be content with their works of art; "*we*, however, want to be the poets of our lives." (*The Gay Science*, p. 170) Create yourself! Create yourself as artists create art! If Montaigne was epochal in his discovery of the formerly unknown continent called the Self, then Nietzsche was just as important in providing a modern impulse when presenting the self as the result of an aesthetic activity, as a performance that could never be substantially or permanently fixated.

---

106 Transl. Josefine Nauckhoff, Cambridge University Press 2001, p. 104. (Nr. 107) Reference will be given in the text.

Memento: 1869, a couple of years ahead of Nietzsche, the English biologist Francis Galton published a book in which he advocates a new science called eugenics: the basic concept is the manipulation of procreation and genetics in order to diminish the proportion of bad humans and to promote good humans. Nietzsche actually took an interest in Galton and he speculates in his notebooks upon some of Galton's proposals: for instance the castration of criminals and syphilitics. It should be added that Nietzsche eventually said no to eugenics: developing an *Übermensch* is in his view a moral and aesthetic task, not a genetic one, and when it comes to genetics, Nietzsche is a proponent of mixing good and bad instead of cultivating the good at the cost of the bad.

The disastrous results of a negative and preventive eugenics are well known from a 20th century standpoint: versions of eugenics have served as an excuse or tool for racial politics, sterilization campaigns, ethnic cleansing. Still, the ideas of a positive eugenics seem to have a new life in contemporary biogenetics, experimenting with new possibilities of manipulating the fetus in order to design exactly the kind of human being that the parents or the genetic manipulators wish to produce. I suppose this kind of human design is so far more a theoretical than practical possibility, nevertheless the idea is beginning to find its way into common knowledge pertaining to what a human being is and potentially could be: human design is rapidly developing from fantasy into a concrete option.

If the idea of eugenics happened to be contemporary along with Nietzsche's bold improvisations of the self as unfinished and dependant on aesthetic performance, then, it seems that the new genetic ideas of human design happen to be contemporary and commensurate with a striking development in the arts over the last 40 years: I am especially thinking of the visual arts and the tendency, from Joseph Beuys onwards, to stylize the self of the artist in acts of performance. To mention only one of many possible versions explicitly prefiguring (and commenting upon) genetic design: the French artist Orlan, whom repeatedly manipulates her body and then presents it as a work of art.

Versions of this tendency are prominent today in the visual arts – one can think of Cindy Sherman, Sophie Calle, Tracey Emin and many others. Interestingly, for me, these versions often verge on literature, in the sense that they stylize the performing self in anecdotal or allegorical or prosaic settings that can be understood as literary adaptations of the prose of reality. Within the strictly literary field also, we meet an army of followers of Nietzsche's recommendation – create yourself! – in the sense that they construct themselves (or their selves) in acts of literary performance. Finally, the eruptive expansion of so-called web-logs (blogs) points in the same direction: in the new medium, the unfinished and undefined self can be presented and developed in a creative mixture of visual and literary aesthetics. The self on the screen has been digitalized and conceptualized and aestheticized: style and design define the being that, according to Nietzsche, was "the animal *whose nature has not yet been fixed.*"[107]

There is no denying that the internet develops both a new technology and a new media-situation. (I have touched upon this when discussing the prose poem in chapter 5 and the photographic and visual expansion in my last Extension). The blog invites a "life writing" that transforms traditional versions of sound, picture and writing into a new "network" with interaction, design and performance as important components. The screen becomes an interface between self and society redefining (or demolishing) traditional distinctions between private and public. This also has new implications for *prose*: the prose of reality diverts and disseminates in new interactions and networks. The tendency of *prosification* merges with the tendency of *aestheticization*.

The tendency (or tendencies) that I have sketched can very well trigger an exhilarating feeling of freedom: if it is up to myself (and also to genetic science and digital and performative capacity) to define myself, it would mean a liberation from what was earlier called destiny. It could push me beyond my limits, making me surpass myself, expand my capacity. Self-fashioning means that the self is no longer a given entity and no longer *one* entity, rather possibilities lie there and potential plurality. Nevertheless, I must add another memento: One consequence would be that the capacities used in the classical definition of the self in writing and in art – I am thinking of memory and historical experience here – are no longer mandatory. The creative performance has no need for memory. Performative experience substitutes accumulated experience. Human design disturbs or obliterates genetic memory. The idea of a private sphere was instrumental for developing the modern writing of the self, from

---

107 *Beyond Good and Evil*, transl. R.J. Hollingdale, Penguin Classics 1990, p. 88. Reference will be given in the text.

Montaigne up until the present – but the performance of the self redefines the private sphere and web-logs eliminate the distinction between private and public. The experiences of negative eugenics during the 20th century should remind us that liberation has a prize. The prose of today and tomorrow may not account for that prize. Such misgivings require modification in a further Extension.

Aesthetic Appearances

The prose of today and tomorrow implicates human design and performance of a digitalized self. Such were the words and misgivings of my last Extension. I shall try to develop this a little further by examining some prominent metaphors of contemporary aesthetics: presence, surface, appearance and network. Again, Nietzsche is called upon to open the discussion that will continue with some contemporary philosophers and close with an example from visual and public art.

Nietzsche on appearances

In the passage from *The Gay Science* quoted above (Nr 107), Nietzsche defines art as "the *good* will to appearance." (*The Gay Science*, p. 104) By stressing the *good* will, he implicates a contrast to the *bad* will that provides us with false appearances (promoted by empirical sciences). The good appearance, artistically produced, makes our existence "bearable." It follows that bad and deceitful appearance makes existence unbearable. (Ten years earlier, in *The Birth of the Tragedy*, he wrote that: "only as an *aesthetic phenomenon* is existence and the world for ever *justified*"[108].) Aesthetics had been given a moral dimension and belongs, in *The Gay Science*, to Nietzsche's more or less "epicurean" strategies. Sometimes it was the right food, sometimes the good climate, now it is art too that should make life "bearable."

In *Beyond Good and Evil*, his thinking on appearance takes another turn, for instance in number 34 (p. 64ff.), starting with Nietzsche scorning all credulous philosophers, that are duped by *not* being duped by appearances, ending with his praise of *fiction* as the truth of existence. Also in *The Genealogy of Morality*, he concludes

---

108 *Kritische Studienausgabe*, Berlin: de Gruyter 1988, 1: 47.

that there is nothing but a great nothingness beyond or behind appearances. The disposition of philosophers to search for truth beyond appearances reveals aversion to life itself and displays a *will to nothingness [einen Willen zum Nichts]*.[109] In one of his last works, *The Twilight of the Gods*, he finally eradicates the distinction that he has been attacking by proclaiming the 'apparent' world to be the only world; "the 'true world' is just a *lie added on to it* ..." Dividing reality into 'true' and 'illusory' is now called "decadence" and the "fact that artists have valued appearance more highly than reality is not an objection to this proposition. Because 'appearance' here means reality *once again*, only elected, strengthened, corrected ..."[110]

Nietzsche used appearance and art in order to solve his problem: the Platonic-philosophical priority of intellect and contemplation. He finally turns "Platonism" upside down. This means that aesthetical representation in a classical and romantic sense – art as a representation of reality – has given way to art as presentation: art as production of new reality. Art as work has been replaced by art as aesthetical practice.

Aesthetic presence

Aesthetics of today is not only a philosophical question, it is also an instrumentation of a social situation, one that I touched upon in my last Extension. Aesthetics, style and design produce identity and indicate a social situation where our lives are submitted to *aesthetizisation*: aesthetical considerations have become important for body, sex, food, home, sports, behavior, identity. In other words, aesthetics has developed in the direction that Nietzsche anticipated and recommended (this is not to say that he would have acclaimed the aesthetizisation of today or even thought that it makes existence "bearable").

Some German philosophers have tried to conceptualize contemporary aesthetical reality: I have borrowed the term *aesthetizisation* from Wolfgang Welsch; Karl-Heinz Bohrer uses the *sudden* in order to describe the orientation towards the here-and-now of sensual perception; Gernot Böhme uses *atmosphere* in his approach

---

109 *Kritische Studienausgabe* 5: 412.
110 *The Anti-Christ, Ecce Homo, Twilight of the Gods And Other Writings*. Transl. Judith Norman, Cambridge University Press, 2005, p. 168 and 170.

to the conditions of aesthetics. I shall, however, turn to Martin Seel, who employs versions of "appearing" – *Erscheinung, Erscheinen* – in order to describe what happens when something makes an aesthetical appearance.[111]

For Seel, the aesthetical experience is a potential in *everything* registered by our senses. The sensual manifestation of reality takes place all the time and Seel therefore devotes his philosophical energy to delimiting aesthetical manifestations from all the others. The most important difference is that we normally use our senses pragmatically, in order to orientate ourselves and then proceed. Aesthetical use make ends in themselves: when we experience that something is appearing solely in order to experience its appearing – then we have undergone an aesthetical experience: "To perceive something in the process of its appearing for the sake of its appearing is the focal point of aesthetic perception."[112] Art and aesthetics is all about making present, to "linger" in this presence and meet it with an attention that is an end in itself. "Aesthetic intuition [*Anschauung*] is a radical form of residency in the here and now." (*Aesthetics of Appearing*, p. 33) The experience of presence manifests time as an interval, as "an *enduring passing away* [*bleibenden Vergehens*]" (*Aesthetics of Appearing*, p. 147) – Seel tests out a paradox in order to describe the temporality of aesthetical experience. He is a good humanist, claiming that this interval, this experience of presence, also means a human meeting, where time, history, humanity and fellow individuals are made present.

With his persistent concentration on the here-and-now of aesthetic experience, Seel competes with some other important contributors to the aesthetics of today, such as Karl-Heinz Bohrer in *Plötzlichkeit. Zum Augenblick des ästhetischen Scheins* (1981) and Hans Ulrich Gumprecht in *Production of Presence* (2004). Gumprecht's title declares his concern. Aesthetic "presence" constitutes aesthetic experience and is certainly not restricted to the arts. It could also be found in watching sport or taking any pleasure. His subtitle – *What meaning cannot convey* – indicates that aesthetic presence, in his view, is pure and instantaneous. Such presence is inaccessible for any hermeneutical version of aesthetics, seeking historical meaning

---

111 *Ästhetik des Erscheinens* and *Die Macht des Erscheinens*, both on Frankfurt: Suhrkamp 2000 and 2007. The former is translated by John Farrell, Stanford University Press, 2005. Reference will be given in the text.
112 *Aesthetics of Appearing*, transl. John Farrell, Stanford University Press, 2005, p. 25. Reference will be given in the text.

and experience through interpretation. Seel cannot accept that. He claims that the here-and-now of aesthetic experience also makes historical time present for our senses. If we can only linger in the aesthetic moment, then we can learn something about time and about our own mortality.

Nietzsche claimed that art presents "appearance" (and he diagnosed the tendency of aestheticization early on). Seel (and others) add that aesthetical appearance is all about the presence of the moment and the here-and-now of time. The concentration on art as surface and appearance has indeed been an imperative in the visual theories of modernism since Clement Greenberg. Even photography (as discussed above) – for a long time considered as the most referential of all the arts – has been digitally transformed from representation into presentation.

This situation in contemporary aesthetical theory tempts me to reformulate my questions from the previous Extension: what happens to memory, history and experience? If art presents the appearance of presence, would it imply that art no longer represents anything at all? Perhaps what is made manifest in the moment of aesthetical presence does not matter, as long as something is made manifest?

I would think that my collected literary examples, as presented in this book, dismiss such misgivings. Instead, they confirm Seel's view of the aesthetical moment as a moment that can give presence to history. Even Harryette Mullen's prose poem, discussed in chapter 5 as the prime example in my collection on pure surface, admits other possibilities. The digitalized surface that I saw in the extension of Mullen's text, is best described as a *network*. The network makes horizontal connections and therefore supplements my main concern: the tendency of prosification. However, the network could also establish relations in time and therefore make history and experience topical. I shall try finally to demonstrate this with a visual example.

I am thinking of the Holocaust Memorial that was inaugurated in Berlin in 2005. Close to the Brandenburger Tor there are 2,711 rectangular concrete slabs, "stelae", crammed into a huge surface of 19,000 m^2. All the stelae seem similar but none is quite like the other. Together they make an enormous "forest" or "network" of anonymous "statues". Many visitors pass continually through this "forest" and part of the idea seems to be that it is physically impossible to walk in a group: you have to make your own way through this "labyrinth."

The architect whom is responsible for the Memorial, Peter Eisenman, has on several occasions stated that the Memorial does not represent anything at all. It represents that which cannot be represented by representing "nothing". (It is quite easy to be reminded here of one of Adorno's aphoristic statements in his *Aesthetic Theory*, previously quoted in ch. 4: "In each genuine artwork something appears that does not exist."[113]) There is nothing behind or beyond these stelae, they are pure surface (emphasized by the anonymous concrete). They manifest an aesthetical appearance that seems impenetrable. On the other hand, it would be impossible to walk through this "forest" happily accepting the here and now of the aesthetical experience. Nor would it be easy to restrict yourself to intellectual contemplation. The network connects all these stelae into a compact surface but also relates it to history. You cannot walk through the memorial to the victims of Holocaust without an interpretative work of your memory. You may imagine that you are walking amongst chimneys or tombstones or in the middle of a petrified army. The work of interpretation had already started when I wrote "forest" and "labyrinth" and "network." The "network" (if that is the adequate word) may even be regarded as a metaphor for what I call prose. Indeed even for what Benjamin expected as the prose of "universal history" (according to chapter 4).

The Memorial is, in other words, a striking example of an aesthetized surface giving a purely aesthetical experience – while not at all in conflict with historical memory. The Memorial makes time and historical experience topical. Everything is appearance. History is not yet finished.

---

113 *Aesthetic Theory*, transl. Robert Hullot-Kentor, London: Athlone 1997, p. 82.

Aesthetics of Prose

"Like a kind of Antarctica, prose remains one of the last undefined, untheorized bodies of writing in early modern European languages." These words of Roland Greene and Elizabeth Fowler[114] aim at the Renaissance but I think they also have some later relevance, and concern today even. In this book, I have attempted a mapping of this territory and in this final Extension I shall summarize my effort in a few points.

- Prose may be undefined and little known. The theory of literature has refrained from prose and restricted the theoretical interest in the essence(s) of literature to poetry. Still, prose is well known to all: the language of prose, as it is read and practiced as well as the reality of prose, as it is lived. Hegel's diagnosis of modern life in modern society, mentioned several times above, as prosaic – the "prose of reality" – soon became a commonplace. It still is. This notion was strikingly put by Emily Dickinson in a couple of her poems. In poem 657, she describes her poetical life as a kingdom of possibilities in comparison to being imprisoned in prose:

> I dwell in Possibility –
> A fairer House than Prose –
> More numerous of Windows –
> Superior – for Doors –

Furthermore, in poem 613 she describes the reality of prose as closure and stagnation:

> They shut me up in Prose –
> As when a little Girl
> They put me in the Closet –
> Because they liked me "still" –

---

114 *The Project of Prose in early modern Europe and New World.* Cambridge University Press, 1997, p. 1.

These poems seem to manifestly be on the side of poetry against prose. Although perhaps not, in the final analysis. Dickinson is using a kind of prose in her poetical statements. Her striking use of dashes functions as a visual installation and a prosification. The dashes are "doors" and it is impossible to say if they open up for poetry or if they "shut me up in Prose" or "put me in the Closet" of prose. They definitely constitute a prosaic ingredient in these poems: they install order and continuity in a world of pure contingency. They indicate the very physics of prose.

- The physics of prose has been presented in many forms and by many metaphors. Montaigne's essayistic body, disparate but still hanging together, never finished, always something to add. Nietzsche's labyrinth, showing by hiding, hiding by showing. Pamuk's Istanbul or Kapuściński's World: diligently mapped by foot and pen. Bernhard's or Sebald's meandering syntax, indicating a state where everything is connected with everything else – together with the insight into the boundless contingency of everything that exists. *Network* was my final metaphor: in the network, everything is as close to the centre as Adorno wished it to be; and as disseminated as it should be for Benjamin. The network connects and includes. It encompasses the world and makes history come alive. It is the physical basis of the metaphysics of prose.

- The metaphysics of prose, as expressed by Walter Benjamin, reaches for universal history, including everything created, not only now and not only in history but also in the future. There is no end to prose. The prose writer has only one obligation: keep writing! It is impossible to decide if this is Dystopia or Utopia.

Index

A
Adorno, Theodor 3, 39, 59, 65, 67–78, 175, 178
Anderson, Mark M. 163
Aragon, Louis 108
Artemisia Gentileschi 135
Auerbach, Frank 161
Augustine 10

B
Banti, Anna 127, 135–138
Barnes, Djuna 108
Barthes, Roland 57, 153, 164
Bataille, Georges 47
Baudelaire, Charles 63, 83–84, 153
Benjamin, Andrew 51
Benjamin, Walter 3, 51–67, 70, 72–75, 78, 82, 91, 94, 175, 178
Berg, Alban 75, 147
Bernhard, Thomas 127, 150–154, 156, 159, 178
Beuys, Joseph 168
Bizet, Georges 39–40
Blanchot, Maurice 35–36, 39, 43, 58–60
Boehncke, Heiner 164
Bohrer, Karl-Heinz 172, 173
Boswell, James 111
Bourget, Paul 39

Bouvier, Nicolas 99, 101, 112–116, 118, 125
Brecht, Berthold 55, 57, 148
Breton, André 160
Burckhardt, Jacob 41
Byron, Robert 99, 101, 110–112, 114–116, 118–119, 125
Böhlendorff, C. U. 73
Böhme, Gernot 172

C
Calle, Sophie 168
Canetti, Elias 99, 101, 112, 123–125, 127, 144–148
Cervantes, Miguel de 99
Cicero 24
Cioran, E. M. 132
Colli, Giorgio 33
Conrad, Joseph 106

D
Dahlhaus, Carl 75
Defoe, Daniel 99
Deleuze, Gilles 34
Derrida, Jacques 35, 47
Dewey, John 51–52, 62
Dickinson, Emily 76, 177–178

E
Eco, Umberto 57

Eisenman, Peter 175
Eliot, T. S. 57
Emerson, R. W. 12
Emin, Tracey 168

F
Flaubert, Gustave 82, 102
Foucault, Michel 104, 133
Fowler, Elizabeth 177
Freud, Sigmund 20
Friedrich, Hugo 45, 59–60, 62, 75
Fussell, Paul 100
Förster-Nietzsche, Elisabeth 32–33, 36

G
Galton, Francis 168
Gautier, Théophile 156
Gnam, Andrea 163
Gogh, Vincent van 52, 58
Gohar Shad 110
Gombrowicz, Witold 127–128, 132, 133–135, 138, 139
Greenberg, Clement 59, 174
Greene, Roland 177
Gumprecht, H. U. 173

H
Hamacher, Werner 30
Hamsun, Knut 156
Hartog, François 104, 121
Heftrich, Eckhardt 45
Hegel, G. W. F. 39, 55, 61, 68–69, 73, 76, 81–82, 156, 177
Heidegger, Martin 36–37, 43, 51–52, 58, 62, 70, 90
Heine, Heinrich 82
Heinz, Manfred 36

Hellingrath, Norbert 72
Herodotus 103–104
Holland, Patrick 104–105
Horkheimer, Max 67
Huggan, Graham 104–105
Hugo, Victor 59–60, 82, 130–131
Hölderlin, Friedrich 52, 62, 71–74, 78, 89

J
Jacobson, Roman 52, 84
Joyce, James 57

K
Kafka, Franz 57, 128, 132, 161
Kapuściński, Ryszard 99, 102–103, 112, 116–119, 125, 178
Kisiel, Thomas 36
Kittler, Friedrich 62
Kowaleski, Michael 100

L
Lacis, Asja 65
Levi, Primo 100
Lichtenberg, G. C. 30
Löwith, Karl 43

M
Magris, Claudio 145
Mahler, Alma 148
Mallarmé, Stéphane 59–61, 65, 84, 91, 93–94
Man Ray 160
Marco Polo 105
Merleau-Ponty, Maurice 82
Meschonnic, Henri 74
Miller, Henry 129–131
Mitosz, Czestaw 127, 138–140

V
Velasquez, Diego 18, 136
Vernet, Thierry 112

W
Wagner, Rickard 31, 38–42, 75
Walser, Robert 162
Welsch, Wolfgang 172
Wilcox, J. T. 31
Williams, William Carlos 84
Woolf, Virginia 108, 160

INDEX

Montaigne, Michel de 3, 9–27, 70, 128, 133–134, 167, 170, 178
Montinari, Mazzino 33
Mullen, Harryette 81, 84, 91, 93–95, 174
Murdoch, Iris 148

N
Nabokov, Vladimir 127, 140–144, 146, 153, 159
Naipaul, V. S. 99, 112, 121–123, 125
Nehamas, Alexander 31
Nerval, Gérard de 156
Nietzsche, Friedrich 3, 29–48, 55, 78, 81–84, 86–90, 103, 105–108, 115, 139, 167–169, 171–172, 174, 178
Nin, Anaïs 127–132, 135

O
Oliver, Kelly 31
Ondaatje, Michael 127, 148–150
Orlan 168

P
Pamuk, Orhan 127, 138, 151, 153–156, 159, 178
Pascal, Blaise 30
Perse, St. John 139
Pessoa, Fernando 46, 62
Plato 13, 16
Pliny 24
Ponge, Francis 84, 87, 91
Porter, Dennis 104
Pratt, Mary Louise 105, 124, 126

Proust, Marcel 57, 76, 111, 142, 147

R
Rank, Otto 129–130
Riedel, Manfred 36
Rilke, R. M. 84
Rodenbach, Georges 94, 159

S
Sackwille-West, Vita 160
Said, Edward 104
Sandel, Cora 99, 107–109, 118–119, 125
Sartre, Jean-Paul 52, 59–62, 133
Schiöler, Niclas 86
Schlegel, Friedrich 75
Schönberg, Arnold 75
Sebald, W. G. 3, 153, 156, 159, 161–164, 178
Sebond, Raymond 26
Seel, Martin 77, 79, 173–174
Seierstad, Åsne 99, 103, 112, 118–121, 125
Sextus Empiricus 11
Sherman, Cindy 168
Sloterdijk, Peter 44
Snyder, John 27
Sophocles 11
Spengler, Oswald 127
Stanley, Henry 106
Starobinski, Jean 17–18
Stendhal 161
Stierle, Karlheinz 57

T
Terence 11
Tranströmer, Tomas 81, 83, 85–91, 93